CHRISTIANITY and BUDDHISM

SINCLAIRE THOMPSON MEMORIAL LECTURE

FIFTH SERIES

BY

THE VENERABLE BHIKKHU BUDDHADĀSA INDAPAÑÑO

PREFACE

"This is glutinous rice" — is a description. "Eat it! you will gain strength!" — is a call to commitment. The latter cannot be intelligible without the former and yet the former would be lifeless unless it is given meaning by the latter. Accumulation of descriptions will not give us strength. Commitment, a total and concentrated response to the call, lies in the deeper stratum of religious life. The committed person has his own language to describe the truth to which he is committed.

Our understanding of the Thai Pali Buddhism is often paralyzed because of our failure to take the dimension of religious commitment seriously. We congratulate ourselves prematurely with our "thorough understanding of the descriptions" of Buddhism assuming that that is the whole of the Buddhist existence. Innocently we still speak of "comparative religions". All attempts, however, in the line of comparative religions is unsatisfactory or even distorting (I am speaking from Theravada Thailand!) unless they reach the depth of "comparative religious commitments". But this enterprise lies next to impossibility since religious commitment is a fire that burns any objective scale by which we propose to pursue our comparison. Yet do we have any other alternative than to try to reach this level of discussion if we want to see and feel the living essence of religion?

This year the community of Chiengmai is greatly privileged to hear in person the famed Buddhist scholar and author, Venerable Monk, Buddhadāsa (meaning, servant of the Buddha) Indapañño as he delivers the Fifth Series of the Sinclaire Thompson Memorial Lectures. Rev. Thompson was aware of the serious spiritual encounter between the Buddhists and the Christians in Thailand. He was not just toying with the "description" of religions called Buddhism and Christianity. He wanted to explore the quality of life and strength of a man who has eaten either Christian or Buddhist glutinous rice. We are about to listen to a committed Buddhist. Only this kind of occasion can truly help us to grasp the unfrozen living Buddhism in Thailand today.

Kosuke Koyama
Thailand Theological Seminary
Jan. 1967.

INTRODUCTION

I am pleased to deliver the SINCLAIRE THOMPSON MEMORIAL LECTURES, FIFTH SERIES, for it will help create an atmosphere of mutual understanding among the followers of both Christianity and Buddhism, and also make people understand their respective religions at the same time, for the audience here is both Buddhist and Christian.

Every human being, no matter to what country he belongs, or what language he speaks, or what religion he professes, has but one universal problem, namely, *overcoming evil or mental impurity or defilements*. That which is called evil or mental impurity is to be found in each individual. It does not belong to or is not the problem of one particular religion only; each individual professing any religion has the problem of overcoming the evil. As such the way to solve this problem must be one which can be used by every human being. The way or instrument to destroy evil is named 'religion,' therefore *true religion or religion in essence is universal in its application.* The belief that there are literally many religions is something meaningful only in the eyes of those who see only the outer forms, or view religion only superficially. There are different outer forms or embodiments of religion, but every religion or what is embodied in different forms of religion is but one and the same thing. If one looks at religion with mundane eyes one will see many religions. If one sees with supermundane eyes one will see only one religion. With mundane eyes one cannot see the essence of religion and this is why one fails to overcome one's evil or suffering.

One cannot judge whether a certain religion is right or wrong, true or false, on the strength of one's study or reasoning, for the criterion or standard thereto must be *"the fruit which one really gets within one's own mind."* Therefore, before passing any kind of judgement with regard to a religion, followers of different religions should first try to obtain the fruit of the practice of whatever religion they delight in. In that case all questions or differences as regards religion would vanish and it will become clear that all religions in the world have one common 'heart' or pith in the same way as all men in the world have but evil or suffering as a universal characteristic.

Religion is *"a system of observation and practice which binds man to the highest thing being therefore the benefit of every human being."* It is through one's own ignorance that one does not know really this highest thing, so it would not be wise to blame that which is called religion. Be wide awake, try to understand first the highest thing and you can easily and undoubtedly approach or realize it. It is hoped that this series of lectures will add, to some extent, to your understanding of the highest thing.

BUDDHADĀSA INDAPAÑÑO

MOKKHABALĀRĀMA, CHAIYA
JANUARY 10, 2510 B.E. (1967)

Publisher's Note

This booklet contains the text of the 1967 Sinclaire Thompson Memorial Lectures presented by Buddhadāsa Bhikkhu of Suan Mokkhabalarama, Chaiya. The set of three lectures was delivered at the Thailand Theological Seminary in Chiang Mai on the 18th, 19th and 20th February, 1967.

Though Sinclaire Thompson was himself a Christian, yet where deeper, spiritual things were concerned he was in no way whatsoever biased against other religions. In fact, he made every effort to help adherents of all religions to come to an understanding of religion in general, and so do away with any form of inter-religious ill-feeling. His real aim was to bring peace and happiness to individuals and society; and he went about achieving this goal by fostering greater inter-religious understanding.

Sad to say, he was obliged to take leave of this world before the hoped-for results had been achieved. Fortunately however, several of Sinclaire Thompson's former co-workers decided to carry on the work he had started. One thing they did was to initiate the Sinclaire Thompson Memorial Lectures. These have been delivered every year since the death of Sinclaire Thompson in 1963, so that this, the 1967 series, is the fifth. Invitations to lecture are extended to people qualified to do so, regardless of whether they be Buddhist, Christian, or Muslim.

As is explained in the lectures, if a person can become so disenchanted with selfishness and egoism that he is able to eliminate them completely from his mind, then he will achieve true inner peace and coolness, and at the same time bring peace and coolness to the world as a whole. This is because selfishness and egoism are the root causes of all sufferings and confusion. If selfishness and Egoism are done away with, nothing would remain but Truth, or Nature, which is not the property of any particular person or any particular religion at all. One could then be said to have penetrated to and attained Truth or Nature, or to have become one with God-the highest, the superlative attainment possible for man.

The lecturer demonstrates that the various religious systems, that is to say the various methods for attaining Truth, or Nature, or God's Kingdom, consist in constantly introspecting into one's own mental condition, so that one eventually comes to realize that the condition in which the mind is free of all selfishness and egoism is in fact its *natural* condition. The confused state in which there arise selfishness and egoism comes about through the intervention of another factor. That other factor is evil, or the *mental defilements*, and is not something peculiar to any particular religion or individual. It comes into existence of its own accord, naturally, and passes out of existence in the same way. When it comes to dominate any person's mind, it produces selfishness and egoism, ultimately bringing suffering and trouble to that individual and the whole of society. Our job, then, is to be on guard, to keep constant watch over our own mental condition until such time as we discover the condition of freedom from egoism. We have to cultivate this freedom from the self-idea by carefully preventing that element called evil or *defilement* from intervening. Selfishness and egoism will then gradually diminish, and in the end will disappear altogether; and this is the highest thing to which man can attain.

We see, then, that all these things–selfishness and egoism, the system of continuous introspection to discover that the mind is naturally free of the idea of selfhood, the element called evil or *defilement* which comes in and compounds matters so that selfishness arises, the technique of being watchful to prevent the mind's becoming confused, as well as the result to be achieved, namely a mind free of selfishness, free of evil or defilements, peaceful, cool–all these are just *Nature*. So the words *Buddhist*, *Christian*, *Muslim*, and so on do not exist for one who has in view the highest goal of life, namely a mind free of selfishness and egoism.

For whatever worth this work may have to its readers, thanks are due not only to the lecturer but also to Sinclaire Thompson and his co-workers, through whose efforts it was brought into existence.

As for the translation of these lectures, it has been done by various hands. The first lecture was translated by the Venerable Puṇṇo of Wat Benchamabopit. The first half of the second lecture has been rendered into English by a christian. The second half of the second lecture together with the third lecture have been translated by Mr. B. Siamwala and Mr. Hajji Prayoon Vadanyakul of the Friend Muslim Mission. Several Western Bhikkhus have in conjunction with Thai laymen checked and re-checked the translation to make sure it would be as near to the original Thai text as possible. However in spite of all efforts some flaws may still be lingering about. It is hoped that they will be corrected in due course in the next edition.

If you are interested in wiping out selfishness, then read this set of lectures. It may help in the job of reducing, and finally eliminating that "self" so as to leave nothing but Truth, or Nature, which is nobody's property, but is just Nature in its own right.

V.S.

Sublime Life Mission
5/1-2 Atsadan Road, Bangkok
Tel. 22549.

THOMPSON MEMORIAL LECTURE

Fifth Series

CHRISTIANITY AND BUDDHISM

by

THE VENERABLE BHIKKHU BUDDHADĀSA INDAPAÑÑO

(First Lecture)

MUTUAL UNDERSTANDING OF EACH OTHER'S RELIGION

Members of the Faculty, Students, and Guests of the Seminary:

To study different religions comparatively, with an attitude of goodwill, results in mutual good understanding. This in turn, brings about a way of thinking and acting in men which causes them not to hurt each other's feelings. And not to hurt one another's feelings further gives rise to peaceful co-existence par excellence between all the societies and nations in the world. It is because of this fact that I am very much delighted to be here and have a chance to lecture on the subject of religion with the viewpoint of comparative studies.

The first point to be discussed for the sake of comparative study is that both the Buddha and Jesus Christ were born in the world to make imperfect things perfect. Jesus Christ said, "*Do not suppose that I have come to abolish the law and the prophets: I did not come to abolish, but to complete.*" -(Matthew 5/17). There are also words of Isaiah about Christ :

"And he will proclaim judgement among the nations.
He will not strive, he will not shout,
Nor will his voice be heard in the streets.
He will not snap off the broken reed,
Nor snuff out the smouldering wick,
Until he leads justice on to victory.
In him the nations shall place their hope." -(Matthew 12/18-21).

These words, obviously apply to the world as a whole or to all the countries in the world, and this accounts for the fact that the religion (of Christ) is international and does not belong to nor is limited to any particular nation. So it should be borne in mind that, as principle, the word of Christ or that of any other saint in the Bible, is meant for the world at large and not only for the land of Palestine.

As for the Buddha, we find him saying, *"The Tathagata, the Perfect One, appears in the world for the gain of the many, for the welfare of the many, out of compassion for the world, for the good, for the gain, for the welfare of gods and men."* -(Mahāsīhanāda Sutta Majjhima-Nikāya 12/37/46). The important point to be remembered here is that the Perfect One was not born to hurt any creature or creed. He was born to make this world perfect, as is the ultimate goal of life. For this reason he did not hurt the feelings of the followers of other religions, but taught what was lacking in those religions, and also explained things anew from the highest level, giving old ideas the profoundest meaning in all respects. Thus he gave everybody a chance to select for himself; there was no compulsion with regard to accepting new insights in religious matters. For example, he gave a new interpretation to the common belief in heaven and hell, which is clearer and also more interesting, so badly needed for practical purposes. He explained hell and heaven as being in the heart of man in this world of ours, these states are not something somewhere outside (in space or time) to be experienced after death.

While comparing Buddhism and Christianity we can see that both the founders were born not to clash or collide with followers of any religion different from their own, for they did not work in their own interest; they preached their doctrines for the sake of the many in the world. They did not deliver their messages for egotistic benefits, but for the weal of all mankind. It is only those with selfish interests who arbitrarily clash with others. Neither Jesus nor the Buddha had the intention of hurting anybody, but they worked altruistically for the sake of perfecting those things which could be achieved by human endeavour. Even if their activities show some revolutionizing effects, they are nevertheless based on truth alone, having in view the welfare of the world. Principally *all the founders of religions were born with the sole aim of making world perfect with the thing that man should attain.* Followers of any religion who do not try their level best to act in accordance with the original aims of the founders of their respective religion, are to be regarded as people who have gone astray.

Now the second point we should pay attention to, is the different ways of expression which are used in the scriptures of each religion. There are two ways of expression, two languages, as it were. The first is *conventional language;* let us call it here *the language of common man.* The second is a special kind of religious language embodying the *"inner world"*, the culture of mind, of the *heart;* let us call this language the *"language of Dhamma".* Both the Tripiṭaka and the Bible are full of these two kinds of language; now many kinds of misunderstanding are due to the fact that many people do not understand *the language of Dhamma.* They take words of Dhamma as *conventional language* and consequently cannot come to any understanding at all. This results in confusion within one religion and with regard to other religions as well, especially when making a comparative study. For this reason I appeal to you to be tolerant, and to try to understand this point correctly. To cut a long story short I shall give some examples from the Bible itself as regards the two ways of linguistic approach.

In Genesis 2/17 God forbids Adam to eat the fruit of the tree saying: " ... for in the day that you eat of it, you shall die." Now here the word "die" is *the language of religion,* i. e. the word does not signify physical death but refers to "spiritual death". Whether it be God or the writer of the Bible, he knew well that at that time Adam did not know the meaning of the word "die". Even if he knew, he knew only its meaning as it is understood in terms of *conventional language,* i. e. physical death. Adam had not yet eaten the fruit, so he had no knowledge of the nature of duality such as life and death, male and female, good and bad, etc. At best, he knew only the literal meaning of the word death as understood by common man.

God, or the author of the Bible, knew that in this case the word "die" applied to spiritual death which in this context is to be taken as the arising of original sin which is responsible for inescapable suffering. So here the word "die" is a *term of "Dhamma"*, and by no means *conventional language.*

In John 3/3 we find: "Truly, truly, I say to you, unless one is born anew, he cannot see the kingdom of God." Now here the word "born anew" is a word from *the language of Dhamma*, i.e. "rebirth" in this very life and not physical rebirth after physical death. The kind of rebirth which is meant here may happen through a complete mental change or revolution: furthermore, we find in the same passage (John, 3/6) very clearly stated: "That which is born of the flesh is flesh, and that which is born of the spirit is spirit." This shows with all evidence that "birth of flesh" is birth in the *conventional* sense, and "rebirth, spiritual birth" is birth in the *language of Dhamma.*

In Matthew 20/28 we find: "He came to surrender his life as a ransom for the many," and in Matthew 19/17 we find the words: "If you wish to enter into life, keep the commandments.". Now you see, the word '*life*' in these two contexts has quite different meanings. In the first context this term is to be taken in the *conventional sense*, but in the second context it signifies the life which knows no death, which is eternal and is to be taken in the spirit of the *language of Dhamma* or that of God.

In some sections of the Bible the same style of language has been used as can be found in the Tao Teh

Ching of Lao-tzu, e.g. in Matthew 10/39: "He who finds his life will lose it, and he who loses his life for my sake will find it.". Here you can see for yourself that the word '*life*' has two meanings, i.e. one meaning in the sense of *common language* and the other stemming from *religious language*. Apart from this single term which is to be understood with regard to the *language of Dhamma* the whole context of the above passage is in the *language of Dhamma*. A person who has never acquainted himself with such *religious language* before, cannot understand it at all. In this connection it is because the word 'life' has two meanings which are exactly opposed to each other.

These few examples may suffice to show that there are different strata of language with different ways of expression in both the Buddhist and Christian scriptures.

The next point is very important and requires our wholehearted attention : It is due to the ignorance of the *language of Dhamma* that one abandons one's own religion and embraces another. If one really understands the meaning of one's religion in the *language of Dhamma*, he will love his own religion just as one loves one's own life. As for Christianity I believe that because the Jews did not understand *the language of Dhamma* of Jesus Christ, they did not take faith in him as the son of God. Even though Jesus worked many wonders, still they did not believe in him, and the so-called redemption or the surrendering of his life as a ransom for mankind took place. *All this throws light on the significance of the language of Dhamma.* If we make a comparative study of religions we should be extremely careful with regard to the precise interpretation of *the language of Dhamma* as far as our own religion is concerned. Only then a comparative study will be of use. If the followers of two different religions positively confirm the stand of their own respective religion which sticks to each single letter and is based on the *language of common man*, there will not be the slightest prospect of coming to a mutual understanding or agreement. On the contrary, such a superficial comparison will result in misunderstanding and disagreement which will lead to disputes and might even breed ill-feelings of hatred. Where there is hatred there is always the potentiality of harming the peace of the world as a whole.

As for Buddhists they can accept all the passages of Christianity as in agreement with the Buddha's teaching, *if they are allowed to interpret the language of Dhamma in the Bible in their own terms*. In the following I am going to show how such an interpretation is feasible.

Please consider that it is the masses, ignorant of the *language of Dhamma*, who are *the greatest enemy of a religion*, no matter whether it be Christianity or Buddhism. Commonly other people (outsiders) or outward things are regarded as the enemy of religion. So far, such an attitude has certainly not rendered religion any beneficial service. On the contrary, it has given rise to many new problems, many abandon religion altogether, many believe ignorantly and feel satisfied only with rites and rituals, many keep converting from one religion to another, many try to propagate their convictions, without any real success, etc.

If you contemplate this point thoroughly, you will see why it is so important to have a clear understanding of the afore-mentioned two modes of expression. That is also the reason why I have taken so much time in dealing with this point. It is the different ways of interpreting *the language of Dhamma* that account for all the schisms and sects in a religion which unnecessarily have an evil effect on religion. The true objective of the founders of all religions with regard to the completion or perfection of what is most useful and needful for humanity is not being achieved, because the followers of the respective religions interpret the *language of Dhamma* wrongly, having preserved wrong interpretations and preached wrongly to such an extent that the world has been facing turmoils and problems created by the conflicts among religions. On this account you are requested to pay special attention to this matter.

Now we come to the third topic dealing with the points of agreement among all the religions, first of all by complying with the principle: "For every nation there is an apostle.". —(Quran,. Chp. 10. Sect. 5, v. 47). It is only by accepting this motto of goodwill on such a high level that there can be a possibility of agreement even as to doctrinal points of secondary importance setting out first on a higher level and eventually also covering more specific doctrinal matters. When there is this kind of goodwill, a comparative study of religions may prove exceedingly fruitful.

An apostle means "a man of God who preaches the truth". The term "apostle" is, in fact, found in every religion, including the teaching of the Buddha. The word "God" (Phra Chao) is a term belonging to the *language of Dhamma* and as such it may be interpreted in various ways according to the feelings and the way of thinking of the followers of different religions. When addressing you here, I (Kha-pa-chao) am using the pronoun "kha-pa-chao". This pronoun is the abridged form of "poo-ti-pen-*kha-khong-phra-chao*" which literally means "the person who is the servant of Lord (kha=servant, pa-chao or phra-chao =Lord or God). This being the case, would you who are Christians be so strict as not to let me have a God like you, belonging to him as it were? How do you think about this? If you are too strict in this matter, our discussion will certainly not be totally fruitful, and perhaps will be a waste of time for all concerned. *Buddhists also believe in God* (Phra Chao), or you may say "Lord" (phra pen chao) *in a Buddhist sense;* and this God of theirs has the same significance as that of others. As to how this is possible I shall point out in detail in my lecture tomorrow. At present I request that you be flexible enough to enhance mutual understanding in a spirit of discovering the truth. If you do not achieve success in establishing Christianity in Thailand, it is because you do not recognize the Buddhists as already having their own God as well.

Thus we should be flexible to the extent that we acknowledge that every group of people speaking different languages and living in different corners of the world, has, without exception, something of its own which has the characteristic of "God". When a given group of people is still in its early stages of civilization, that group will have a limited understanding of what is called "God", or their conception of God will be in a primal stage of evolution. *But we should not think that their conception of*

God is wrong nor should we take the extreme of not granting them any conception of God at all. Nevertheless, their conception of what is called God will evolve and mature to perfection. It is our duty to help further this evolution in the spirit of the words of Jesus quoted earlier "I have not come to abolish the law ..... but to complete it".

As for preachers, they may be prophets or apostles who have achieved what should be achieved by them. They preach the truth about God which is suitable as for their place and time, although they may not always use the manner of expression to which the common man is accustomed. We can, however, expect that the essence of their message, as regards the truth, is the same. Even if there are at times verbal discrepancies, the spirit of their preachings has nonetheless the identical objective of achieving the best thing man can eventually achieve. When people fail, and commit sins in the present they are to regard them as lessons granted by God so that they may lead their lives properly in the future. One's bitter experiences alone are effective enough to alter the course of one's mind towards discovering new ways which will ensure that one does not undergo unpleasant experiences endlessly. The preacher of truth helps to find out such methods in a comparatively short time, and indeed this is something worthwhile. This is the best a preacher can do for a troubled mind, i.e. reducing the time-element to the minimum length; for every person is to take due time in accordance with the law of learning lessons by experience, before he will be able to find his way out of the trouble. God or, if you like the word, nature, has created man to think freely and to make his own decisions.

On this ground let us all use the working hypothesis with regard to the validity of the statement that *"There is an apostle for every nation."*.

Now the next point which requires flexibility and a willingness for mutual understanding is the fact that nowadays people study their respective religions in a way which may be compared to *"climbing a tree starting from the top."* which is quite contrary to the way of "climbing" in the days of the Buddha or Jesus, for at that time the way of approaching truth was like *"climbing a tree by starting from the foot of the tree"*. To explain, nowadays we have mountains of scriptures by our side, both the text and the commentaries thereof. We study religious literature with weary and dewy eyes to such an extent that our heads are full of ready-made facts seen from various angles, say, from the viewpoint of religion, philosophy, literature, etc. And this manifold knowledge of ours, with reference to the scriptures, fails to enable us to effectively choose what suits us best and in which we can take refuge. *The more we study the scriptures the less we know of the essence of religion.* As a matter of fact *the essence of religion can only be reached by genuine practice alone.* This is what is meant by "climbing down a tree from the top" as it is practised nowadays in every religion. As for the men of olden days, they had no scriptures whatsoever, or we may say that they were virtually illiterate before they started treading on the way of religion. When they set out they progressed gradually only after having understood just one or two points of a verse pointing at the truth. And thus they could reach the essence of religion in the same way as one "climbs up a tree starting from the foot of the tree". For this reason all of us in the world should be broad-minded and willing to recognize and cope with this state of ignorance which is widespread among the people, whether they be conscious of it or not. Interpretations of any religious point tend to be different, so much so that we get more and more separated from each other, possibly even to the extent that we shall at times begin to develop feelings of hostility towards each other. It is because different people have their heads stuffed up with facts reached at from different approaches. Everybody stresses his own particular viewpoint. Be assured that if Christianity would have been introduced in India in the days of the Buddha it would have been welcomed warmly as "friend-religion" or "brother-religion", because in those days people were broad-minded enough as to firmly believe in the principle of these *three paths to emancipation:*

1. the path of "paññādhika" with the wisdom-factor predominating:
2. the path of "saddhādhika" with the saddhā-factor (confidence, trust) predominating:
3. the path of "viriyādhika" with the willpower-factor predominating.

One may select any of these three paths according to one's individual temperament. Buddhist even nowadays accept this principle which is just in conformity with the nature of human beings and which the Buddha has pointed out. If one thinks impartially with an unbiassed mind everybody will agree that *Buddhism tends to be "paññādhika"*, *the path with the wisdom-factor predominant, that Christianity tends to be "saddhādhika", the path where trust or faith predominates, and Islam "viriyādhika", the path where will-power is predominant.* Thus each of these three religions has one of the three paths as its special characteristic. But strictly speaking, none of the above religions provides only one of the paths mentioned; each religion comprises all the three ways; the only difference is that a certain religion may give preference to one way or the other, as e.g. in Christianity the way of faith is given preference before the other ways as has been said above. As to how the other two ways of wisdom and will-power may also be found in Christianity will be explained later. Presently it is sufficient to point out that each religion does have all the principles of truth (Dhamma) which man requires, such as trust (faith), will-power (energy) wisdom, loving-kindness (mettā), generosity, selflessness, egolessness, etc. If we want to know why a particular religion stresses, or prefers this or that point, then we should take into account to whom, when, and where a religious teaching or sermon was given. We should know to what kind of people, under which circumstances, and at what places such teachings were given. In this connection, however, let us all be careful not to allow the knowledge we get through *"climbing a tree starting from the top"* to cover the true facts. Let that knowledge not be a barrier in the way of compassion and broad-mindedness as far as the adherents of each religion are concerned. Let that knowledge not be a hindrance on our way of co-operation and peaceful co-existence, let us stand on our way of performing our duties in accordance with the right objectives of the respective religion.

In our world as a whole and within a considerable length of time, in a particular place and period man needed the *way of faith*, and in another place and period he needed the *rational approach* (demanding the cause-and-effect-principle), and yet in another place and period people required the way of controlling the mind or the use of *strong will-power*. Now in our age the three paths of religious practice have, due to modern communication (which have rendered the world increasingly limited,) come into contact with each other. Is it then befitting for us to quarrel with each other with regard to the purpose of nature or God? In my way of thinking, all religions can meet on a common platform provided that there is an element of mutual broad-mindedness and goodwill. While depending on environment and circumstances, it does not matter which particular kind of way among the three paths of practice one religion prefers, regarding the other paths only as complementary. But when there is a contact among different religions, the three paths can merge smoothly in the same way as streamlets coming from different directions flow down a mountain and intermingle forming one single stream which fertilizes abundantly, certainly more than a single streamlet can, the land it flows through. *The more broadminded and tolerant the believers of different religions are towards each other, the more fruitful religious life will be, the more the world will be blessed by God.*

The next topic for which a sympathizing flexibility and willingness to understand is required regards the interpretation of religious terms such as *God, Dhamma,* "*religion*", *Karma,* "*Emancipation*", including "*way*", "*fruition*",

"*Nirvāṇa*" down to the simple word "*world*". Let people of different religions be allowed to interpret religious terms in line with the language of Dhamma, which is different from the literal language of the common people. To interpret in the spirit of the Dhamma-language will be most rewarding for the world, never otherwise. To state this point precisely, we should maintain that if *an interpretation of any word in any religion leads to disharmony and does not positively further the welfare of the many, then such an interpretation is to be regarded as wrong; that is against the will of God, or as the working of Satan or Mara.* I positively wish to say that if an interpretation of any word in any religion and in any assembly where adherents of different religions meet, is given *keeping in mind the good of the many as the sole aim* without being too rigidly attached to traditions which are always subject to change, then there will be no possibility at all of its being wrong or against the will of God. In reality however we do not show very much of this enlightened flexibility with regard to Dhamma-Interpretation, and are quite at variance with one another. Different people adhering to different religions follow tradition handed down over hundreds of generations so much so that people often do not know the essence of their religions; and this is *due to different interpretations of the term "belief or faith", all being inconsistent with the will of God. Thus we should be extremely careful with interpretations of a rigidly traditional nature.*

If among the followers of religions there is enlightened flexibility as regards interpreting in order to arrive at an agreement, then such a kind of interpreting *will firmly stand against any anti-religious element as a whole.* In this era we have to regard dialectic materialism as an anti-religious philosophy. Some reasons for this are as follows: As religious institutions have given wrong interpretations to certain religious tenets, different religions consequently are not in harmony with each other. Furthermore because of wrong interpretations people fail to apply themselves to religious practice so that their so-called 'religion' ceases to be an effective device for solving the problems of daily existence. Only when a religion has failed to do its duty does materialism come into existence in the world. Once having made its appearance, materialism begins to uproot religious life as a whole. But, conversely, if religious institutions interpret the tenets held by them correctly, especially the tenets expressed in the language of Dhamma, then religious practice itself will prove to be the " decided opponent " of materialism in all forms. It will thus destroy its very roots leaving no chance for further growth in the future.

For this reason adherents of each religion in the world are required to be tolerant and cultivate sympathetic willingness to understand each other when coming together. They are required to be ready to interpret the main tenets of their particular religion in a way that is agreeable to adherents of all other religions so that finally all the believers of different lands, speaking different languages may actually and in all respects find (in those unifying interpretations aiming at the very essence) the answers for the problems of their lives. To take such a step would be in accordance with the purpose (will) of what we call *"God"*. We are to firmly stick to the fact that *"God"* has given us the way which *is correct and complete in all respects, but we ourselves have interpreted that way wrongly,* and consequently the result of this wrong interpretation is that God, so to say, is still to try humans by giving materialism a chance to reign the world for a certain time until humans are definitely tired of it. Let all students of religious truth be compromising with regard to interpreting different tenets of religion with a view that all religions in the world may be welded together for the common cause of getting rid of the confusion which is engulfing the whole world. This will encourage men to apply religious principles to the solution of their problems in all respects and in all walks of life, be it politics, economy or any other sphere including, of course, the spiritual cultivation of heart and mind.

The last topic which requires enlightened flexibility, and broad-mindedness deals with the unwillingness or reluctance to commonly use some conventional religious terms. For instance, Buddhists generally hesitate to use the word "*religion*" for their religion (Buddhism—the doctrine of the Buddha), reasoning that the word "religion" is used for a theistic system of belief in God and prayers, while the teaching of the Buddha has nothing of this sort, not knowing, however, in what sense and in how many senses the term "God" in the language of Dhamma is meant. Further they do not know that the word prayer has manifold levels of meaning, both shallow and deep, even including a system of practice which may be based entirely on self-help. This kind of praying in the sense of self-help is based on the fact that each individual tends to think dualistically, i.e. thinking that there are always two "halves", as it were, two aspects of personality in an individual person. These two "personalities" are generally known to us as good conscience and bad conscience always struggling with each other. If in this case the expression "self-control" (restraint) or "deceive ourselves" can be used, one can use the term "pray to ourselves" with good reason. This too is a kind of praying to God which is moreover used by most people for the simple reason that we call "God" what is generally thought of as goodness.

As for Christians they would perhaps be quite unwilling to use the term "Nibbāna" so common to the Buddha's teaching for what they call "Salvation". And they would try to argue that the two, Nibbāna and Salvation, cannot be the same thing in any respect. They may insist for instance that Salvation is only to be granted by the grace of God and not through the practice of the Noble Eightfold Path of Buddhism. But I wish to point out that *the Noble Eightfold Path is what is called "Dhamma" and Dhamma is nothing but God.* What and how this all is to be understood, will be explained in detail in my lecture of tomorrow.

Another most important term to be understood is "revelation". Christians believe that revelation, no matter whether it was bestowed by God through Moses or upon St. John through Jesus, is a revealing insight directly granted by Heaven. Buddhists would not use this term in Buddhism, holding that such a phenomenon (revelation) is quite alien to the teaching of the Buddha. But as a matter of fact this term can be found everywhere in the Buddhists scriptures. For instance in the Udāna the Buddha is given as saying: *When the Dhammas reveal themselves to a brāhmaṇa* (religious man, man of practice) *who is striving hard in meditation, then all his doubts are dissolved.*" This means that when a person earnestly and devoutly ponders on something with a highly concentrated mind, for a sufficiently long time, then Dhamma-truth which has the characteristic of light appears to him in an unusual way, so much so that we must decidedly call it for its being exceedingly extraordinary something beyond the approach of the common worldling or regard it as the divine coming from Heaven. After all, the word "revelation" simply means " the *revealing* of something in an unusual way", and as such, it can be found in all religions. We should therefore not have any aversion to using this term to signify an insight into the divine as is shared by all men of practice in every religion. All this illustrates that the important terms such as "revelation", etc., which are traditionally supposed to belong exclusively to one religion can be commonly used, that we can commonly use the other less important terms as well, provided that there is no unwillingness to sympathetically try to understand each other, nor that there is by any means derision or grudge which are against the *commandment of God*.

To sum up this topic on broad-mindedness we can say that it is the "officials" of different religions who have interpreted their respective religions out of selfish motives without showing any flexibility so as to make people believe that *there are different types of religions with different ways and goals* rather than only one unique way. Because of this, people have begun to think that there be many a "God" (the really authentic one of one's own religion and the unauthentic ones of outsiders) rather than one "divine truth" to be shared by all. Arbitrary interpretations are responsible *for the group-feeling among men. People do not realize that humanity as a whole is one single unit*, or that all men are "descendants of one person", etc, etc.   Jesus did not call his religion "Christianity". We ourselves classified his teaching as "Christianity" after his death in an effort to separate them from all the other religions.   Jesus did teach the way leading to the "Kingdom of God" addressing all men in the world. The Buddha as well did not name his teaching "Buddhism". The Enlightened One called the way of practice he taught **BRAHMACARIYAM**, the Holy Life, as found in the Vinaya Piṭaka e.g.: "Brahmacariyaṁ pakāsetha - proclaim ye the Holy Life." He never used the word religion-doctrine. We ourselves have labelled his teaching "Buddhism" and we have tried to be separate from other religions, deeming it authoritative to have something special not found in other religions. The Perfect One said: "Proclaim ye the Holy Life, glorious *in the beginning* (for people of comparatively low wits), glorious *in the middle* (for the average people of common understanding), and glorious *in the end* (for people of a highly developed sharp intellect) according to the letter and meaning (spirit) *for the good of gods and men*". Such being the case, let us think for a while whose fault it is that there is now disharmony among the followers of various religions, who by following contradictory interpretations bring discredit to each other, to the extent that all religions have become weak and have hardly any reserves left to effectively resist for the common good all the anti-religious elements in our midst.

As for the fourth topic of our comparative study we shall deal with the item entitled *"Christianity from the point of view of Buddhists".* The first and foremost point to be understood is the fact that *every religion has an outer covering.* This means that various rites and rituals have been imposed on religion due to special circumstances, environments etc. Undue stress on outer form has given birth to rigid traditional teaching, including dogmas added by different churches according to individual ways of thinking for the purpose of suiting individual tastes, and which have finally been reduced to mere rituals. As time passes these outer forms cover the essential core of meaning making it vague or invisible. Therefore religion for the masses merely contains outer forms of religion such as rituals etc. which are in most cases in line with instinctive needs and sublimated devices manifesting desire. This is evidently revealed by such acts as making merit e.g. when donating a little sum of money and thereby expecting in return a "reservation" in some celestial abodes. In this way when blind faith takes possession of the heads and hearts of people it becomes difficult to distinguish between religion and superstition. *Personally I have listened to talks of some Christian missionaries which were recorded and broadcast on radio saying that Buddhism is a teaching which teaches men to worship "spirit houses" and promulgating occult arts, etc, etc.* It may sound very funny indeed, for all of you sitting here know so well that all such things as worshipping spirit houses and occultism have nothing to do with the Buddha's teaching at all. Nevertheless one might wonder, why these things were imposed on

Buddhism. It is these elements which are *a covering—indeed something more than a mere covering—and which some Buddhists, followers of that religion only by name, do practise;* this is why many people misunderstand Buddhism completely. Moreover when 'Buddhists' perform such superstitious practices for a long time people tend to despise their own religion, consequently they embrace Christianity which is comparatively new to them and has no *such* superstitious practices. In doing so *they are never going to correctly understand the Buddhism which they previously professed. This is the fault of the covering of true religion.* Therefore before making a comparative study of religions we must be sure that the religions to be compared must be clearly seen in their pure form without the outer coverings. Also the points to be compared must be taken from the textual sources of the respective religions; if some points, however, are taken for consideration from commentarial literature then they should always be in conformity with the original canonical works.

Before throwing light on the Buddhist attitude towards Christianity it would not be out of place to say a few words about *the meaning of the* word "religion" alone in the Buddhist sense, without specifically referring to any religion such as Christian religion or Buddhist religion.

The term 'religion' has been interpreted by people in so many ways and on so many different levels that it would not be possible to enumerate all to them here. We will therefore consider the term only *in a way necessary for mutual understanding* between enlightened Christians and Buddhists. We will use the scientific method as the basis for our comparative study. We will here agree to the common usage of the word 'religion' wherever and whenever the word 'religion' is implied. But in the very beginning we should decide once and for all as to how far we are justified in using this word commonly for both the religions.

Western scholars themselves are of different opinions as to the root of this word 'religion'. It seems that old literary works anterior to the era of Cicero held that the word 'religion' was derived from the root 'lig' which means "to observe" in the sense of observing and then practising in accordance with "God's revelation". In this sense then religion is a system of practices leading to the highest objective which a man is capable of achieving. Buddhism as well has the same characteristic, that is it is a way of practice which leads to the state where there is no suffering at all.

In the days of Servius scholars considered 'religion' as having its root in "leg" which means 'to bind' in the sense of binding a man to the highest thing, i.e. God. Such being the case, Buddhism too is a religion because it is the means for binding man to the highest state which is a state of complete extinction of suffering, called by Christians "Kingdom of God" and by Buddhists "Amata-Nagara", the "City of the Deathless" etc.

In the days of St. Augustine we find scholars synthesising both roots "lig and leg", in order to give religion a more appropriate and complete meaning. In this way the connotation of the word 'religion' implied the ways of *practice according to the Commandments which bind man to the highest, namely God.* Likewise in this sense Buddhism is a full-fledged religion, i.e. it is a perfect way of practice which when followed completely binds man to the state in which he knows of no suffering and which is variously named Nibbāna, Parama-Dhamma, the Deathless, etc. having the same meaning as "Kingdom of God."

Buddhists can accept categorically the above mentioned meaning of the word 'religion' without taking any exception. They also hope that every religion in this world is meant for this purpose or objective. It does not matter if methods of practice differ. As said elsewhere methods are bound to be different due to environment, time, habits, mentality, temperament, etc. of people. We may safely say that the one 'God', if he taught *twenty-five centuries ago in India, nineteen centuries ago in Palestine, and nearly fourteen centuries ago in Arabia* could certainly not teach in identical terms. How can we then expect the scriptures of different religions to be identical in each letter? The Buddhist way of thinking which is called Dhamma and which becomes clear to the man of long-standing practice (brāhmaṇa), quite naturally tends to be different in certain matters of secondary importance. This holds good particularly when a discovery of truth is made in far-away lands and at different times separated from each other by many centuries. But when coming to the very essence of religion, that is something identical and contained in all religions, the essence being not to cherish self-love (egoism-selfishness) but Dhamma-love devoted to the truth, or you may say God-love. Not to cherish self-love (selfishness) is truth; *it is in the highest sense the*

Summum Bonum, and we cannot say that it is something Buddhist, Christian or Islamic; for this reason selflessness in the Christian sense implies the same thing as is understood in Buddhism or Islam. And it is in this sense that the state which we call selflessness (absence of selfishness) is *truth. It is the truth of all places and all times.* Where there is no being to think selfishly for its own sake that is the essence of all religions. (When there is no *self* to think for *it-self* in a *selfish* way there is found the essence of all religions.) When there is no self which owns things for itself then thanks to such a realization one naturally belongs to Dhamma or in other words, to God. Man can therefore reach God or Dhamma, the ultimately genuine, by treading the common way of getting rid of self-love or selfishness.

The above is all about the thing known as '*religion*' from the point of view of the followers of the Buddha or those who have studied facts in the same way as Buddhist have by relying on sound reasoning and wisdom of insight which one can realize and prove for and by oneself.

Having dealt with the meaning of the word 'religion', we will now refer to *Christianity from the standpoint of Buddhists.* To save time we will discuss Christianity with reference to what is known as "the Bible". We take for granted that the Christian teaching is contained in the Bible and that the two (Christian teaching and the Bible) cannot be separated. First we will therefore give thought to what is called the "Bible".

When talking about the Bible, however, it may be mentioned that we make use of the same eclectic approach as Buddhists do in reference to their scriptures (by not regarding all the texts as equally authentic); we may thus eave out the Old Testament by not discussing it. Why so? Because in the Old Testament there are merely accounts and stories of the creation of the world and other events in the world of the Hebrews right down to the birth of Christ. As you know, there is no teaching of Jesus in the Old Testament. As for the New Testament one may say that the teaching of Jesus contained therein is enough or more than enough to guide man on his way to emancipation. Upon this account we may leave the Old Testament unconsidered to save time and to devote it to the teaching of Jesus.

My personal opinion is that *Christians in the days of Jesus* could practise according to the teaching of Christ to gain the highest Fruits without caring for the lengthy Old Testament. The same holds true in the days of the Buddha when *many a man realized the Noble Path and obtained the Noble Fruition without having anything to do with what is known as 'Tripiṭaka'*. The Tripiṭaka was compiled after the Mahā - Parinibbāna of the Awakened One. (Passing away of the Buddha) A very remarkable fact as regards the Tripiṭaka is that it is many times (about twenty times) bigger than the whole Bible (including the Old Testament). It is a record of practical teachings and methods in multifarious variations directly aimed at extinction of suffering. As for the Bible in the first instance it is the New Testament containing the teaching of the practice leading to emancipation. And thus only one fourth of the Bible contains the actual teaching of Jesus. Short as it is, it is enough or more than enough for the practical purpose of emancipation. I, therefore, dare say that Christ himself might have forbidden his disciples to be very much concerned with the Old Testament which was perhaps even less extensive at that time than nowadays for the purpose of study and practice. I will point out later my reasons for making this statement.

This kind of prohibition on the part of Jesus is the same thing as the Enlightened One, too, out of practical considerations discouraged his disciples from discussing impractical 'problems' such as: "Is a 'person' reborn after death or not? 'What' is it that is reborn? — How is one reborn?" To futile speculation like: "Is the world limited or not?", he gave no answer as is stated in the Māluṅkyovāda Sutta of the Majjhima—Nikāya. Even such questions as: "Are there gods? Does heaven literally exist or not? Where is heaven?" were also regarded as irrelevant by the Compassionate One. He called such useless questions "unanswerables", ABYĀKATA. But time and again the Master insisted upon making such enquiries as: "From where and how do different kinds of mind-oppressing suffering arise? What is it that gives rise to suffering? What is its direct cause?..." He pointed out that answers to such enquiries can be got directly through spiritual experience.. He declared that in one's own experience one will see by oneself that all kinds of suffering or spiritual death result from one's inability to reach Dhamma or God. By Dhamma or God, however, one is to understand here "Absolute Truth". That absolute and universal truth is: " *Wherever and whenever there arises a feeling that self belongs to self resulting in selfishness there and then arises suffering. But when there is no such feeling, that is, when self belongs to Dhamma or God, then there arises no suffering.*" When a man of practice reaches the stage of attainment where he is able to destroy his feeling in terms of self and selfishness, he is freed from suffering. For here and now he is above suffering and therefore contented and satisfied; he need not enquire whether after death beings are reborn or not, where heaven is, etc. although these are age-old questions. He does not bother about these questions because the happiness which results from the destruction of the feeling and the engrained idea of self and selfishness is incomparably superior to that kind of happiness which is said to be experienced in the various heavens. In this stage of experience he categorically puts an end to egoism, hence no ego-self is left to die or to be born or to suffer. There is left nature alone which is by itself without any death or birth. This state of experience is, translated into conventional language, the attainment of the *Deathless* (AMATADHAMMA) or *God.* Everybody should clearly understand that at *any time (whether within a moment, an hour or even a day) when there is no feeling whatsoever of self as belonging to self, we have reached and become one with God.* This is possible because ignorance or attachment which gives rise to the feeling of self and which works as a covering is put to an end at that time. Hence the illuminating rays of God or the Absolute Truth (Parama Dhamma) enlighten our hearts and minds, which is in fact a universal phenomenon. He who is one with God will be given at that moment a new life or another type of life which is totally different from the previous one. If this can be achieved on the highest level (i.e. in the absolute sense) then it is to be known as freedom or emancipation, that is once and for all, emancipation from the world of the flesh. For such a person who has attained this state of emancipation there is nothing left to be done, his religious practice is completed. This is the direct way, and requires no waste of time in studying unnecessary things. One should only study that which is necessary and try to solve problems of immediate concern. One should practise to gain the highest fruit without delay. Let one study only one single point as to how to get rid of craving which is the mother of I-ness and My-ness so that one's mind becomes pure. I am fully convinced that the founders of religion without exception *had enough compassion for their disciples and followers to save their time by not allowing them to study unnecessary things.* Even the short message as contained in the few pages of the Sermon on the Mount in the book of Matthew is far more than enough and complete for practice to attain emancipation. There is no need to take into account even the rest of the New Testament, not to mention the Old Testament. I wish to say directly that the Christian ' officials ' who preach Christianity in the street, and on the radio do not know how to select the essentials for their messages. It is the same with the Buddhist monks who teach simply the general covering or outward form of Buddhism. They do not grasp *the essence of Dhamma. This essence is not to have attachment to anything whatsoever in terms of I and My (I-ness and My-ness).* In the Mahāsāropama Sutta,

Mūlapaṇṇāsa, Majjhima—Nikāya, the Buddha says that the core of BRAHMACARIYA, the Holy Life, is emancipation, Vimutti, which is the same as salvation; wisdom (Paññā) is the sapwood surrounding the pith, meditation (Samādhi) is the bark around the sapwood, morality (Sīla) is the outermost dry rind, and finally gain, honour name and fame and even heaven are but the fallen sere leaves. What is generally taught or what people are interested in these days is not very much concerned with the essence or core of religion. That is why people of different religions are scattered and not in harmony with each other. *In our comparative study of religion we should compare religion straight-forwardly without being considerate of any body.* I hope that all of you will pay special attention to this.

Both in the Tripiṭaka and the Bible there are many parts which need not be of interest for anybody and which may be left out. The only exceptions are those who are 'officials' whose duty is to teach, and others who want to be well-versed in the scriptures from the literary point of view. As to this once the Buddha taking a handful of leaves said: *"Things known to the Tathāgata are as many as leaves in the forest, but things I teach are comparatively only equal to this handful of leaves"*. As for Jesus Christ, he too had little to say. And this becomes very clear if we observe the fact that even to the twelve foremost disciples and apostles Jesus taught a few words, and did not resort to lengthy discourses. The same thing holds true of *"God"*. Revelations granted by God, whether to Moses, Abraham or others including even Jesus, were but in a few words. It seems that the only thing needed was *faith and practice.* As for the scriptures which were compiled and revised later on, they have become so voluminous that it causes quite a headache to go through the whole of them. As a result of this, modern scholars have their heads so full of different scriptural facts that they find themselves *lost in the jungle of the scriptures.* In this respect both the Tripiṭaka and the Bible fall into the same category. Why so? Because to go through the whole of the contents retards progress to be made by a person who wants to realize the essence of religion as quickly as possible. It is necessary to convene a meeting of the leading personalities of the respective religions to discuss religion anew in order to bring into focus again what is needed most for life. This thing required for a meaningful life should be made known to the people in a convincing, befitting and up-to-date way, appealing to the people of this modern world of material progress.

Having so far given thought to the word 'religion' we are now going to take into account Christianity in comparison with Buddhism.

The first question we will take up for our consideration is: In which respect do the two religions differ? In this respect the Buddhist first of all will ask whether Christianity teaches self-help or relies on external help rendered by anybody else. He would also like to know the meaning of help given by another. If the taking of another's help means acting according to another's advice, would that be called self-help or help of another?

According to what we are generally told we may briefly say: That Christianity contends that everything depends on the will of God. We cannot help ourselves without the help of God or without his consent. Buddhism, on the other hand, maintains: We are to help ourselves, we are to act by ourselves. And by doing so we receive the fruits of our own actions. There is no God to distribute the fruits of our actions apart from the Law of Karma. *If there be any God he would be nothing but the Law of Karma.* In this way there is no personal God who lives somewhere in heaven and controls the destiny of beings. To put it in conventional language we may say that Christianity is a religion which relies on external help, whereas Buddhism teaches the way of self-help. Thus there is, ordinarily speaking, no possibility of their going together. *But speaking in the language of Dhamma or from the view-point of absolute truth by keeping in mind the truth hidden in between the letters or behind the sound of speech, there definitely is a possibility of blending.* And how? In the language of Dhamma God and the "Law of Karma" are one and the same thing. Such being the case *both religions can well go together as far as the essential is concerned.* They differ only in the usage of the words 'God' or 'Karma'. Buddhists affirm that Karma is not something personal helping us. If we do the work which is to be done properly keeping in mind the Law of Karma we receive the result accordingly. Doing evil the result will be evil according to the same Law. Even if one misunderstands good for evil and evil for good and acts accordingly, the result will be good or bad according to the Law of Karma. One reaps the fruits as one acts no matter how one interprets the action. In this way we help ourselves by acting in accordance with the *Law of Nature or Karma which is always straightforward, sure, and impartial; it wields absolute power.* As the Law of Karma is absolute and unbiased we can name it God as well. To see this with reference to Christianity we may say that God, through whom we harvest the fruits of our actions, undoubtedly is no other than the " All Mighty — Law of Karma" of Buddhism. As such we elevate "*Karma*" which means the " *Law of Karma*" which is but the law - nature ruling the world. On this account we call Buddhism "the religion of Karma" or "religion of Self-help".

As for Christianity some preachers have emphatically and categorically declared that one's action will bear fruit, but only when God is satisfied thereby and has the will to let the actions bear fruit. Some even go so far as to say that no matter what and how much good you do, you can by no means receive the fruits thereof unless you act having faith in God. One cannot, they add, be saved only by accepting the Law of Karma which is " thought out by man ". One can only be saved when one has faith in God. They further say that it is God and not the Law of Karma or action done according to the Law of Karma, which guides us on our way. As to such statements, Buddhists could reply: "Christianity is a *"religion of faith"*, or a " *religion invoking external help* "; Buddhism encourages people to think freely. Buddhists can therefore heartily and promptly accept that *God is equal to Karma (God is Karma).* (This statement in practice is, equally true of both religions) But as for Christians, they dare not or have no freedom to think freely on this subject.

Therefore they cannot agree that Karma or the Law of Karma in Buddhism is the selfsame God of Christianity. As a result of this, Christianity and Buddhism take different routes, the former takes the way of invoking external help and the latter prefers the way of internal help. After all, it is humorous, indeed, when it appears that *the underlying truths which make man receive the fruits of his actions are one and the same!*

Now we shall view things from another angle. We Buddhists sometimes think over and discuss such questions as: every religion, without any exception, which is being taught and practised has two levels according to two kinds of people, those of slow and weak intelligence and those of a sharp and keen intellect. Of these the second kind, whose way of thinking and practice is to be regarded as creditable, have certainly attained the right understanding necessary in judging the correct modes of religious practice. If Christians monopolize the truth, insisting that it be found only in their religion and not letting people use their own brains, but having them just believe, then would not their followers be only half-baked? We have heard Christian missionaries teaching in the street and on overseas radio programmes. They only speak of faith over and over again. They shut the door of Christianity, not admitting those who rely on self-help. We do not believe this to be the genuine attitude of Jesus. For thus Jesus has said *"I am the way and you are to follow the way"*. This was said in the same manner that the Buddha taught us to follow the way, i.e., *to practise and follow in his footsteps*. In any event the tyep fo Buddhism which is taught in beautiful pulpits and halls is also all about belief, *belief in heaven.* The practice of the Noble Eightfold Path which is the very essence of Buddhism is hardly ever discussed. People are not overly encouraged to use their own brains for discovering facts for themselves. When attending a sermon or lecture, most of the audience are already strong believers with regard to what is said; so the result is, that while attending a sermon, people half sleep and half listen. While making a comparative study of religion in order to be fair, *it is necessary to compare things on two levels.* For this purpose, on the one hand, we will have to consider Christianity as taught to an uneducated laity or on overseas radio stations as matched with the type of Buddhism taught in fanciful pulpits and in beautiful halls; on the other hand we have to mention and compare those members of both religions who are earnestly trying to understand the teaching from the Bible and the Tripiṭaka itself. And then *correct interpretations should be given both in terms of common language and language of Dhamma as mentioned above.*

We should now try to decide on categories of religion, i.e. to decide as to which category a certain religion belongs. We should decide that if a certain religion has such and such characteristics it be named such and such, etc. As a rough outline we may suggest that the following are the main types of religion:

1. Religion of Miraculous Power and Magic — based on fear on the part of its followers.
2. Religion of Faith — merely based on Faith and Prayer.

3. Religion of Karma — based on the self-help principle.
4. Religion of Wisdom — based on free thinking (reasoning).
5. Religion of peace — based on non-harming oneself as well as others.
6. Religion of Loving Kindness or 'Love' — based on giving up all and everything (for others) etc.

There being several categories of religion, all the followers of a respective religion can easily find out what kind of religion falls under what category. Let us see whether a certain religion falling under only one of the above categories, is satisfactory and complete or not. We should also mark what special characteristics are held to be necessary for all religions.

Before proceeding further I should like to draw your attention to the meaning and implication of the word 'religion' once more. As has already been examined, 'religion' means "a system of observation and practice which causes a person to be bound to God". In this sense, the very virtues of observance and practice are general characteristics common to all religions, or all "dynamic spiritual forces" known as religion. Observation is Wisdom. To practise means action or Karma. On this ground any institution which is to be accredited as a religion must be endowed with Wisdom and Karma (the Law of Karma). Wisdom and Karma must always be the basis or background of religion. Such being the case, how can we decide which religion is to be given what name among the above mentioned six categories? The answer is that, leaving aside the basic characteristics of religion (Wisdom and Karma), we should only take into account the most predominant characteristic of a particular religion and name it accordingly. If a religion is predominantly characterized by Wisdom or Karma, we should notice that Wisdom or Karma is given double stress or that Wisdom or Karma has two levels—the level forming the basis and the level forming the very essence which is predominant in that particular religion.

Obviously, every religion has Wisdom (observation) and Karma as its basis. Yet there is certainly no religion which has only one characteristic mark - Wisdom or Karma - as its basis. Everybody with common sense can see that even a religion of miraculous powers and magic involves action, demanding practice on the part of its followers; so do religions of faith, of peace, and of loving - kindness. Action presupposes observance and again observance is in itself an action. Intentional action is called Karma. Principally we should recognize here that *all religions in the world have something in common which is the very backbone and essence in terms of Karma or action (or practice). Karma or action is indeed the very 'religion itself.'* By action is meant the practice which brings man into relationship with God. It does not matter whether that which is called God is conceived of as a person, or as a power, or as a condition. The only characteristic required of what is called God, is that it signifies the extinction of suffering. That much is quite enough: or just enough; for if we expect more than this it would naturally be tantamount to building castles in the air, which is an irrelevant and unnecessary undertaking.

Now in the course of comparing Christianity and Buddhism, the question arises as to *in which way the two religions are different or similar, and whether a person can be both a Christian and Buddhist at the same time.* Before answering this question we must decide first of all, under which of the six categories each religion falls.

If we take into consideration the level of thinking, feeling, and practice of the aforementioned ill-informed and of those with weak intelligence, then not only Christianity but every religion is reduced to a religion of faith. But if we have the Bible in our minds and think in the Buddhist spirit of reasoning, we feel that *Christianity like Buddhism, is a religion of Wisdom and Karma.* and that *having realized the essence of both religions, we can be both Christians and Buddhists at the same time.* And what is more we can be Muslims or Hindus at the same time. I will explain this later from the Buddhist point of view, which is characterized by Wisdom (Paññā) or reasoning.

We do not feel that Christianity is a religion exclusively composed of faith as is suggested from talks given on the radio or from pamphlets distributed in the streets. But we feel that Christianity is a religion of Karma (action), Wisdom, love (Mettā), and self-help. Now these characteristics of Christianity will be explained in the following way:

The reason that I think Christianity is a religion of Karma is based on my Biblical reading, as follows:

First of all we have Simon (Peter) answering Jesus: "....*thou hast the words of eternal life.*" (St. John 6/68). We Buddhists feel that *eternal life cannot be gained simply through faith*. It (eternal life) can only be gained by practising according to the teaching of Jesus Christ who taught wisely, carefully, and with subtlety. And it is only after one has tasted (through practice) the taste of eternal life, that one may use the word 'faith'. Unless a person has gained eternal life, it cannot be said that he has perfect faith. Apart from this we feel that the thing which is called *"Eternal Life"* is to be taken in the language of Dhamma. Its meaning is deep and it can be understood only by a man of wisdom. Eternal life is too deep to be understood on faith alone. If one does not understand it in the ultimate sense, than how can one long for and appreciate it? Although previously Peter was only a fisherman, he was wise enough to know of a kind of life which was quite different from his ordinary life. He actually realized another kind of life, which made his previous existence non-essential and meaningless. This knowledge must have been very clear to him, and that is why he could understand eternal life. This signifies that "Eternal Life" cannot be taken on faith but is something concerned with wisdom leading to the ultimate goal.

In John 6/63 Jesus himself says, *"It is the Spirit that quickeneth, the flesh profiteth nothing: the words that I speak unto you, they are spirit, and they are life."* These words have no meaning or serve no purpose if one just believes them without understanding. For these are words expressed in the language of Dhamma to **be understood** by a man of higher wisdom. It is only **after** one has become wise enough to comprehend the meaning therein that one can practise accordingly. If a person accepts these words in the language of common people, learns them by heart and also believes them without the spirit of enquiry, then it would be an extremely blind belief or faith. Such a person could not be called a Christian. *Whether certain words will be both spirit and life, depends on correct and noble practice.* And this practice requires even more care and attention than the most technical subjects of our atomic age. In this context, spirit does not mean mind in a general sense. And life as well, does not mean life in the ordinary sense. But there is the eternal which knows no death. I therefore hold that such words cannot be found in a religion based on faith or prayer.

What is generally known as faith, does in fact imply a concentrated mind which results from activity with clear comprehension and earnest aspiration for something higher. In Matthew 21/21 Jesus says: "... if only you have faith and have no doubts ... you need only say to this mountain, 'Be lifted from your place and hurled into the sea, and what you say will be done." In Matthew 17/20 Jesus says the same thing in somewhat different words: "... if you have faith no bigger than a mustard-seed, you will say to this mountain, 'Move from here to there', and it will move; nothing will prove impossible for you." And in Matthew 14/32 we find Jesus catching hold of Peter, saving him from sinking in the lake, and blaming Peter for having little faith. Now we must mark that in these cases faith is not just a passive state but a most active, highly concentrated state of mind. Therefore the type of faith which God requires can never be blind. To believe in an authority blindly, without acquiring the *right understanding* of what is God, seems to be impossible in the teaching of Jesus Christ. How is it possible that we may love others and destroy our selfishness, simply through faith in another's words, but without knowing why and for what and whose purpose we do so? Will such faith be powerful enough to move mountains? The word mountain in this context, interpreted in the Buddhist way, implies the *selfishness* which hinders us on our ways to reach God. This kind of mountain is heavier than ordinary mountains on the earth which are in fact in constant motion. Buddhists have faith as well. They believe that we can 'move these mountains', in order to reach 'God' in a particular sense. A religious system like this should not, therefore, be called a religion of faith. It should rather be called *a system of action to be practised with the highest wisdom concerning God (Divine Wisdom).*

Again in Matthew 6/14-15 Jesus says: "*For if you forgive other the wrongs they have done, your heavenly Father will also forgive you...*" This shows quite clearly that Christianity requires more than a system of prayers or faith in order to attain emancipation. *We must perform actions, (e.g. forgive others) and only then can we free from our wrongs or, as it were, we can "compel" God to do his duty and forgive us.* For Buddhists, such a way is a way of action and not of prayers. This is the system according to which one should help oneself first and then God (or Karma) will necessarily assist us. (God helps those who help themselves.) Forgiving others their wrongs means that we actually want to be benefitted thereby and, note, not just to please God. Buddhists say that by such an act we certainly help ourselves; and we feel that such kind of self-help is surely to be found in Christian teaching. But different interpretations must have been given in different eras and under different circumstances until finally the whole practical teaching has been characterized as based on faith and prayers. We should, therefore, take the Bible as the authentic record of the Christian teaching and not any traditional teaching of the Church, etc. for further comparative study.

In Matthew 7/18-20 Jesus pointed out in a parable that *a person is recognized as good or bad by his actions*. This fits well in Buddhist teaching. In Matthew 6/33 are found these words: "*Set your mind on God's Kingdom and his justice before everything else, and all the rest will come to you as well*," If we take this statement superficially it *appears as something to be taken on faith* or to be a matter of devotion based on faith. *But according to the Buddhist way of thinking deals with the phenomenon of personification, the fact is not regarded as such.* Interpreted in the Buddhist way, the expression, "*Set your mind on God's Kingdom and his justice before everything else...*", implies total sacrifice which is in Pali *Patinissagga*, literally 'giving up'. To explain further. when one has not yet set one's mind on the Kingdom of God one has a feeling of possession with regard to natural things belonging to nature or God, if you prefer the term, one has attachment to natural things in terms of I or My. If that attachment is very strong, that feeling of I and My, too, becomes so strong that one becomes the personification of egoism. But now when setting one's mind on the Kingdom of God one must give things back to God or Nature by harbouring no attachment or sense of ownership. If one can do this, one will gain emancipation, peace, and happiness which is eternal and absolute. We name God 'Dhamma,' or 'nature' which is absolute and always just. Giving up things which one previously thought as one's self and one's own is the most proper and just thing to do for the simple reason that those things actually do not belong to anyone. Even our minds and bodies are in fact not ours; they belong to Dhamma or God. *The mind which is free from the the feeling of self or ego is the mind which has reached God or Dhamma in the highest sense. This state of mind, free from the feeling of egoism is called LOKUTTARADHAMMA, the supermundane.* In the light of this interpretation we feel that this statement concerning the setting of one's mind on the Kingdom of God is the Christian teaching on the supermundane level. We hold that such an act is not mere *'faith';* it is called *"Karma" or action* on the highest level which is characterized by complete cessation of suffering. When one has attained this state when there is no suffering, there is nothing left for one to do, and one is therefore free.

In Matthew 7/2, we find: "*...and whatever measure you deal out to others will be dealt back to you*", which seems to be perfectly in harmony with the Law of Karma in Buddhism. As for the Passive Voice in the quotation you should know *by whom* the same measure "*will be dealt back to you*". Obviously *by whom* does not mean here your neighbours who exchange goods with you. But here according to the language of Dhamma *by whom implies God in the sense of Law of Karma.*

Again the statement in Matthew 7/12, "Always treat others as you would like them to treat you" is but the Law of Karma of Buddhism. If we want to make God love us we must love God first. If we wish to make God do to us what we wish, then we must do first what God likes. This actually means that one must act properly *according to the Law of Karma regarding it as God, the Absolute, the Almighty.* Whether we believe in it or not, the way we act will determine the fruits we receive. This can be regarded as the self-help principle as well.

Matthew 7/7, "Ask, and you will receive; seek and you will find; knock, and the door will be opened...". From the Buddhist point of view, this too is the Law of Karma: In operation it is we who *are to ask*, it is we who are *to seek*, it is we who *are to knock, and it is only when we do so that God is moved to respond.* Mere faith is not enough. Even if one does a lot of sitting and praying, still that will not be enough. Note that the word 'ask' in this context, implies an earnest effort (striving), that is to say, we ask the Law of Karma in the language of practice and not in the language of mere words and sounds.

In Matthew 11/29 Jesus says: "Bend your necks to my yoke...". This shows very expressively indeed that one is to take up the burden of action (practice), in order to be safe and gain emancipation. It does not mean that one is just to take the trouble of putting forth faith. It is rather an admonition to be active and persevere, which is again the Karma-principle in the Buddhist sense.

In Matthew 12/33 we find the statement: "*Either make the true good and its fruit good, or make the true bad and its fruit bad.*" This is again *the Law of Karma as found in Buddhism and also in other religions teaching the Karma-principle*. (The wording of Matthew 12/33 is identical in British and American editions). Therefore, to view Christianity with the eye of a Buddhist, *Christiantity is a religion of Karma* in the same sense as Buddhism is, and it cannot be a religion of faith.

In Matthew 12/50 it is stated: "Here are my mother and my brothers. Whoever does the will of my heavenly Father is my brother, my sister, my mother." Note that in this statement the word "*does*" has been used and not the word "faith", faith in God who is the haevenly Father. This shows that *Jesus demanded action (practice) rather than faith*. Faith alone would not make a person his brother, sister, or mother. Jesus refused to accept Mary as his mother and his own brothers and sisters as his relatives. But he accepted as his sisters, brothers, and mothers, those who did the will of his heavenly Father. Thus this statement, carrying so much weight, stresses practice and not faith or prayer.

In Matthew 18/35 we find: "And that is how my heavenly Father will deal with you, unless you each forgive your brother from your hearts." This shows that *what is known as love or forgiveness has nothing to do with faith.* But it is 'action' to be done from one's heart or with intention. As such it has to be considered in connection with the Karma-principle.

In Matthew 19/17 we find the instruction: "...*but if you wish to enter into life, keep the commandments.*" Here the word *keep* stands for practice. To keep the commandments or *practise according to the commandments, something is needed apart from mere faith in the commandments or in anything else.* Thus the Christian and the Buddhist teachings are alike insofar as the stress on practice is concerned. According to both religions, it is not enough to have faith or a feeling of devotion without any action done wisely. I think that the quotations here cited, are clear enough for you to notice the fact, that even the book of Matthew with comparatively few pages contains many points· which are in agreement with Buddhist teaching. If we take into consideration all the books of the New Testament, think then how many points concerned with the Karma-principle would be found?

To summarize, the Christian teaching of forbearance, forgiveness, helping others, loving others as oneself or more than oneself is quite in keeping with the Buddhist teaching based on practice and not on faith alone. Whether a person understands God or not, does not matter, for, *if one practises these virtues the result will be the same in accordance with the Law of Karma which is, as*

Buddhists know so well, God personified. Even the simplest devotional prayer is to be regarded as a kind of action for the simple reason that one has to do it with one's body, speech, and mind. Thus, all bodily, verbal, and mental actions can be found in an act of devotional prayer. And even the phenomenon of faith can be a kind of wholesome mental action *provided that one's faith is of the right kind based on understanding.* It becomes a wholesome mental action *because it springs from intention, i.e. the very intention to find out a refuge for oneself* with an undeluded mind. Blind faith however, based only on rumour and hearsay, cannot be regarded as karmic action in this case.

We will now consider Christianity from different angles in order to find out what other points apart from Karma and the self-help principle the Buddhist and Christian teachings have in common. The next point to be considered is whether *Christianity is a "religion of Wisdom"* or not.

Again in Matthew 18/7 we find these words: *"Woe to the world for the temptations to sin,"* or in some editions, *"Alas for the world that such cause of stumbling arise..."* This illustrates that the Christian teaching requires wisdom or light to guide one's way; or in other words, if there is a competent guide in whom one should have faith, *that Guide is no other than the Light of Wisdom. God is in this case, the Perfect Light. To believe in God is to follow the Light of God or the Light personified as God.* Generally, faith presupposes another person, as it were; but if *there arises faith in oneself that faith is transformed into light at once.* As for light or wisdom it all depends on oneself: To be really above *temptation* or causes of stumbling depends on the light within oneself rather than on faith in the guide. To interpret this in a Buddhist way, *the wisdom - element can be found in the teaching of Jesus Christ in full measure.*

Matthew 13/23 has: "But the seed that fall into good soil is the man who hears the word and understands it, who accordingly bears fruit, and yields a hundredfold, it may be, sixtyfold or thirtyfold." Please, take notice, Jesus says, "who hears the word and understands", he does not say, "who hears the word and believes" A Buddhist would say, *"Jesus wants a follower who understands the word he hears and not just believes what he hears."* And why he wants such followers becomes clearer in the light of Matthew 13/20-21 where it is said: *"The seed sown on rocky ground stands for the man who on hearing the word, accepts it at once with joy; but as it strikes no root in him he has no staying-power, and when there is trouble or persecution on account of the word he falls away at once."* This shows that one who understands the word and is well-established in the teaching, cannot be otherwise, than firm. But he who believes too quickly is like the seed on rocky ground which is dried up in the sun and bears no fruit. On this ground too, from a Buddhist viewpoint one feels that *Christianity as well is a religion of Wisdom.* And the officials teach nothing but faith over and over again; the result is that some persons whose forefathers were Christian, have abandoned their previous religion and have embraced another, or in some cases they have no religion at all. I have spoken with them and feel that *had not too much undue stress been laid on faith such a situation would not have arisen.*

Matthew 7/45 has: "*... or how can you say to your brother, 'Let me take the speck out of your eye', when all the time there is that plank in your own? You hypocrite. First take the plank out of your own eye, and then you will see clearly to take the speck out of your brother's.*" This is quite in agreement with what the Enlightened One says in the Dhammapada:

> *One should first establish oneself in what is proper,*
> *Then only should one instruct another;*
> *Such a wise man will not be reproached.*
> (Attavagga, 2)
> *As he instructs others so should he himself act,*
> *Himself fully controlled, he should control others;*
> *For difficult, indeed, is self-control.*
> (Attavagga, 3)

Here (Attavagga, 3) the expression "so should he himself act" obviously means "so should he himself instruct" which in turn implies in the light of the second verse that one should first be established in the virtues in which one is going to instruct others. To explain now what Jesus has said, it should be noted that the removal of ones own "plank" is something which involves wisdom rather than faith. If this is regarded as the principal teaching of Christianity, it is a religion of Wisdom as well. In this sense it is up to God *to take the plank out of one's eye;* in the same way as for Buddhists it is Wisdom that performs the same act.

Now we will take up the point dealing with freedom of thinking or reasoning in the spirit of the Kālāma Sutta in Buddhism.

In Matthew 12/13 Jesus is reported as saying: "...So it is lawful to do good on the sabbath." This Jesus said when the Pharisees, upholders of the ancient Hebrew religion, showed according to their sect, their strictness in holding the view that nothing should be done on sabbath, in this case even objecting to the healing of the sick. Jesus did not agree with the kind of strictness they demanded. He taught that everything for the weal and good of the many could be done on a sabbath. This is identical to the Buddha's advice, not to go by mere traditional belief (mā paramparāya - in the Kālāma Sutta, Tīkanipāta, Aṅguttara-Nikāya) which is in the very spirit of the Buddha's teaching. While arguing with the Pharisees Jesus declared: "I tell you, there is something greater than the temple here" (Matthew 12/6); then he added: "For the Son of man is sovereign over the sabbath" (Matthew 12/8). Jesus maintained that he had enough reason not to follow the ancient tradition based on misunderstanding. He wanted to help the Pharisees to get rid of their superstitious practices. And this is why he made his statement, even though the sabbath is regarded as the day of God, and observed as the Holy Day. Jesus, Son of Man, spoke in the name of God, for he wanted to condemn the hypocritical devotion to God and teach the people how to use their brains. But the Pharisees were too blind to understand, and therefore they laid a plot to do away with him. A Buddhist would appreciate *this attitude of free thinking on the part of Jesus Christ* and regard the Christian teaching as an example of free-thought.

According to Matthew 15/1-2, 11 when Jesus was approached by a group of Pharisees and lawyers from Jerusalem with the question: "Why do your disciples break the old established tradition? — They do not wash their hands before meals", he summarised his answer in this way: "A man is not defiled by what goes into his mouth, but by what comes out of it." Then on being asked by Peter, Jesus explained the meaning: "... But what comes out of the mouth has its origins in the heart; and that is what defiles a man. Wicked thoughts, murder, adultery, fornication, theft, perjury, slander, these all proceed from the heart; and these are the things that defile a man; but to eat without first washing his hands, that cannot defile him." (Matthew 15/18-20). This throws light on the fact that, like Buddhism, *Christianity is not a 'religion of rituals'* emphasizing outward forms or superstitious practices. Unfortunately, the latter developed so many forms of ritual covering the essence, that they have become the dominant content.

Jesus had no regard for the ordinary relationships of father, mother, brothers as understood in the language of common people; but, as has already been mentioned (Matthew 12/50), to him whoever does the will of his heavenly Father is his brother, his sister, his mother. By this he wanted to show that he had gone further than tradition to reach the highest truth of religion. This attitude of Christ, with regard to lineage, points to the same Buddhist attitude of *being reborn in the family of the Noble Ones* (Ariyāya jātiyā jāto), and thereby having father, mother, and brothers in another sense. This should be regarded *as living a life characterized by living with wisdom on the highest level.*

Now after having dealt with Christianity as a religion of wisdom, we will take up for our comparative study other characteristic points of great importance and interest.

In Matthew 19/21 Jesus says: "*If you wish to go the whole way, go, sell your possessions, and give to the poor.... and come, follow me.*" To do this means *to live a homeless life*, without any permanent house, without family and without money. *This was the way in which Jesus lived and he persuaded his disciples to lead the same sort of life.* So that they might not have any family-bondage as a hindrance on their way to emancipation. The importance of this type of life is illustrated by him in a parable as found in Matthew 6/25, "No servant can be slave to two masters..." This means that a person either can be rich in this world or win the Kingdom of God. One cannot be rich in this world and also win the Kingdom of God at the same time. To state this clearly Jesus says: "I tell you this: A rich man will find it hard to enter the Kingdom of Heaven. I repeat, it is easier for a camel to pass through the eye of a needle than for a rich man to enter the Kingdom of God." (Matthew 19/23-24). Even if a rich person makes merit, he does so in order to be still richer rather than for the sake of Nirvāṇa or the Kingdom of God.

The above mentioned references affirm that in Christianity a homeless life characterized by renunciation of the sense-pleasures in order to attain the state of perfection is considered the highest pursuit. In Pāli it is known as Nekkhamma or Nekkhamma-Pāramī. Needless to say, Jesus himself was an outstanding example of this sort of life.

One of the most important characteristics of Buddhism is the Middle Way. It means the way of practice avoiding sensual pleasures on the one hand, and on the other avoiding self-torture or self-mortification. It stands for the golden mean, according to which one should have enough bodily and mental strength to perform one's duties on earth. Jesus was in favour of the golden mean, he lived it and taught or persuaded his followers to live it as can be seen in Matthew 11/29-30: "Bend your necks to my yoke, and learn from me, for I am gentle and humble-hearted; and your souls will find relief. For my yoke is good to bear, my load is light." This shows that Christianity upholds the principle of the golden mean to be applied wisely, avoiding the extreme of being too loose or too strict in attitude and conduct. This falls in line with the Middle Way of the followers of the Buddha, a principle of the greatest importance.

Now we come to a subject of a very subtle nature, that is: "*Dhamma is to be realized by oneself*", in Pali: **Paccattaṁ, or in other words, "Dhamma is to be understood and realized within by turning inward, in Pali: Ajjhattaṁ.** Buddhists hold that it is a sober fact known to the wise that there is "*no need to accept or to* *refer to any authority, be it one's own teacher, or one's own scriptures, or even some trustworthy person* (Kālāma Sutta, Aṅguttara-Nikāya). Christ's teaching as well is in agreement with this principle, for Jesus says: "As the Scripture says, 'Streams of living water shall flow out from within him.'" (Matthew 7/38). This means that any person who believes in him by practising and following in his footsteps, would drink the water of eternity from the streams of living water flowing out *from within*. Now practice to be applied here must be the same as in Buddhism, that is to say, *one is to get rid of the life of flesh* and thus enter the divine life which belongs to the nature or God. When one has achieved this one will taste sublime peace and inner calmness. To re-phrase this in Buddhist terms, the achievement would be called *Nirvāna which is the extinction of suffering previously existing in oneself*. The Buddha says: "*The world, the cause of the world, cessation of the world, and the path leading to the cessation of the world—all this has been pointed out by the Tathāgata to be found and realized in this fathom-long body with perception and consciousness*" (Rohitassa Sutta, Aṅguttara-Nikāya). We can find everything in the body; depending of course, on what and how we practise. Even God or Jesus Christ or the Grace of God in terms of water of eternity, etc.— *all can be found in one's own body through one's own practice*. On the contrary, Satan or manifold suffering which is called the flames of hell can be found in oneself according to one's actions. If one practises on the highest level one can find the Kingdom of God within oneself, but it all depends in which way or on which level one practises. *Whether one believes or not, whether one is ready to rid oneself of the life of flesh or not* — this is the whole question; on this question depends whether one is going to be reborn in the Kingdom of God which is, of course, within ourselves, or whether one is going to be drawn in hell which is, as just said, in one's own body, too. In this way the Buddhist principle that Dhamma is to be realized by *oneself* and *within oneself* — (Paccattaṁ and Ajjhattaṁ) can also be found in Christianity.

Whether it is "to be born anew" in John 3/3 or "entering life" in Matthew 19/17, it all implies the mental activity within ourselves here and now in this world. This is to be understood in the light of the Buddhist principle of PACCATTAṀ and AJJHATTAṀ. In the same way other terms or expressions such as "entering the Kingdom of God" etc. have similar implications.

A most striking comparison occurs when we examine *the last words* spoken by the Buddha and Jesus to their disciples; Jesus says: "*Go forth... and teach them to observe all that I have commanded you. And be assured, I am with you always, to the end of time.*" (Matthew 28/20). The Buddha says: "*The Dhamma and the Discipline (DHAMMA — VINAYA that have formulated and taught you will be your teacher in time to come after my passing away*". (Mahā Parinibbāna Sutta, Dīgha—Nikāya). Then he concludes, "All things are subject to decay, strive with diligence." (-ibid). At the time of physical death both the Buddha and Jesus showed eagerness to make their disciples take up their practices earnestly and firmly. They *affirmed their continued being in their respective disciples, in the sense that the Dhamma is perpetuated in the minds of those who practise it.* According to Christianity, this state may be called "living by the spirit or divine". This state for Buddhists means *"to live according to Dhamma - Vinaya which is always in the mind, and is characterized as the purity, brightness and abiding calm of the follower.* The passage, *"I am with you always, to the end of time."* is to be taken in the language of Dhamma and care should be taken to interpret it in the most reasonable and appropriate way. The right criterion of a reasonable interpretation will be that it makes everybody see the Buddha or Jesus as really living with us all the time. Please take it seriously, and you will see that *all this holds true of every religion.*

Another point to be remarked in connection with *the last words of Jesus is that he stressed the practice of his teaching for his disciples and common people,* and not faith. This shows that *faith* means to *follow* on the ground that if one does not follow no result will be achieved. And if it were not so, Jesus would not have used the words, *"teach them to observe".* "Faith" is merely a preliminary action or the first step of practice; *to have faith (and nothing more) means only part of practice.*

When his passing away drew near, Jesus stressed the propagation of his teaching on the part of his disciples in all nations, of the world. As for the Buddha, we know that he began to stress the necessity of spreading the Dhamma by sending his first sixty disciples (each in a separate direction) to preach a few months after his Enlightenment, i.e. in the very beginning of his preaching career which lasted for forty-five years. Both the Buddha and Jesus cherished hope and wished to give light to all people in the world. This is common to both of them. Jesus says: "Go forth therefore and make all nations my disciples; baptise men everywhere in the name of the Father, and the Son, and the Holy Spirit." (Matthew 28/19). As for the Buddha he uttered these words: "Go ye, O Bhikkhus, and wander forth for the gain of the many, for the welfare of the many, in compassion for the world, for the good, for the gain, for the welfare of *gods and men*. Proclaim, O Bhikkhus, the Doctrine glorious, preach ye a life of holiness, perfect and pure." (Mahāvagga, Vinaya-Piṭaka 4/39/32). Whenever truly religious men practise their religion in the most perfect way, it can be said that both Christianity and Buddhism are *universal religions* as deemed by their founders. All this depends on sincerity *towards the founders* of their religions, or towards the Dhamma which is the very religion itself; and in their being devoted to their respective religion, so that there remains nothing more of self-interest or self-importance.

This lecture has dealt with a comparative study of Christianity and Buddhism from different angles and with varying approaches. We have considered Christianity from a point of view *which nobody seems to consider any longer*. This has been done in the interest of correctness and impartiality.

Now to summarize we may say that the whole talk given today falls under five broad categories:

(1) *The founders of all religions in the world were born to help man to achieve perfection of which he is in need.*

(2) All religious scriptures are written in a two fold language; the language of common people and the language of Dhamma. If we fail to interpret the scriptures in terms of the Dhamma-language, different religions will seem to oppose each other and we will be unable to establish a lasting harmony among them. If the language of Dhamma is not interpreted comprehensively and intelligibly some may feel dissatisfied with their own religion and embrace another, or may abandon religion entirely. In addition, if points which belong exclusively to the language of Dhamma, are mistakenly interspersed with the language of the common people, they lose their practical implications.

(3) *Broadmindedness is an essential factor* which cannot be dispensed with while making comparative studies of religions with a view towards good results for the world at large. For example there should be an agreement on such points: that there is a preacher of Dhamma (truth) from God to be found among all peoples of different nationalities speaking different languages; that people today study their religions in a manner which can be characterized as climbing a tree starting from the top or putting the cart before the horse and thereby are lost in the jungle of scriptures; that the criterion of right interpretation of any doctrinal point should be its usefulness for the common good of people in the world; that there should be a terminology of technical religious terms common to all religions so that people may study religion easily and quickly.

(4) *While comparing Christianity with Buddha-Dhamma* it must be acknowledged that each religion has both its outer form and inner essence. In order to be fair we should compare the outer forms of one religion with the outer forms of the other, likewise the inner essence with inner essence and not otherwise. The word religion should be defined as "*a system to observation and practice which binds man to the highest thing*, call it what you will - God or Nirvana. In the New Testament there are many points in agreement with Buddhism or the Tripiṭaka which account for the Buddhist attitude towards Christianity; namely that *the latter is a religion of action and of self-help based on wisdom*, and not a religion based on mere faith as is generally understood. This fact can be proved practically by showing that if Christianity were a religion categorically based on faith or belief, without any other significant characteristic, Jesus Christ would not have laid special stress on action or practice of the commandments which is found everywhere in his teaching; and again he would not have stressed in his last words, "..... and teach them to observe all that I have commanded you.....".

(5) Therefore both the religions are religions of action—to be done by oneself, and of the fruit to be reaped from within oneself and by oneself. It will be possible to achieve the desired harmony, if one lives up to Dhamma, or to put it in Christian terms, "*if one follows the will of God*". In this way both religions are in agreement in all respects; this point will be further explained in the talk of tomorrow.

END

of

FIRST LECTURE

(DEALING WITH MUTUAL UNDERSTANDING OF EACH OTHER'S RELIGION)

THOMPSON MEMORIAL LECTURE

Fifth Series

CHRISTIANITY AND BUDDHISM

by

THE VENERABLE BHIKKHU BUDDHADĀSA INDAPAÑÑO

(Second Lecture)

FATHER, SON AND HOLY SPIRIT

Members of the Faculty, Students, and Guests of the Seminary:

In this second lecture comparing Buddhism and Christianity we will consider the Father, the Son and the Holy Spirit. The word Father as we use it refers to God as the Creator, the Preserver and the Destroyer of the world. We will consider these terms both from the point of view of conventional language (the language of common man) and religious language (the language of Dhamma or Dharmic Language).

I. "GOD" IN ITS GENERAL MEANING

From the distant past long before they received Buddhism until the present day, Thai Buddhists have had a god. This must be understood clearly before we can make any further comparisons. The word "Phra chao" is truly Thai and refers to something which one fears and must beseech or flatter, an instinct among all thinking beings. Before receiving Brahmanism the Thai people believed in some kind of "God" in terms of spirits or divine beings as do all unsettled peoples. When they met with Brahmanism in the present land of the Thai they took over Indian culture including Indian gods such as Siva and Vishnu. During some periods, the Brahmins taught that the kings were incarnations of God. When the Kings died shrines were built for them to dwell in as Divine Beings. The word "phrachao" began to be used for the King. This was the origin of the first person pronoun "Khaphrachao" or the abbreviated form "khapachao". When the time came and the Thai people received Buddhism as their religion the trend towards Brahmanic thinking resulted in glorifying each King as a Buddha. This was something like deification in the sense of Brahmanism. So the first person pronoun "Khaphraputtachao" (Khaphra*buddha*chao) came into use which in its abbreviated form is also "khapachao". Thus the very use of first person pronoun in Thai gives evidence of belief in a god which might be in the form of man, be a divine being higher than man, might refer to what is ultimately the highest of all, or might refer to some power which is so far uncomprehended. The meaning would depend on the level of education, culture, or the way it was intended to use the word. But the real meaning in all cases is the same, that is, the highest which one must fear or beseech as we have already said. A child will have one kind of god and an adult another, a well-educated man another, each according to the concept that will satisfy him, or according to his education. Therefore, that which is called "God" is neither strange nor new to Thai people. And even though there may be novel elements introduced in order to win their hearts, yet their feeling about God and their interpretations of God remain the same as before.

When the words God or Jehovah or the Lord Jesus are introduced to the Thai people who already have a God of their own, they, therefore, do not become particularly interested. So other means are introduced in order to arouse their interest in the new religion, such as education, medicine, or help in making a living. This is why some people become interested and are glad to receive the new religion because not only do they receive some benefit from it but they also feel themselves to be up-to-date, for it gives prestige and fits in with western culture which they think to be more advanced. Yet the word "Phrachao" for such people still has its old meaning and only the name has been changed. Such people know God only in the sense of "person" according to conventional language. They do not yet know God in the true sense of the word. They do not know that God is neither a person, nor mind, nor a spirit. They do not know that *in the religious language* God means Dhamma or the power of Dhamma which is self-existent according to Nature.

As long as man still holds that God is a person, as we think of "person" in conventional language, so long will man not know the real God, and so long will there be disagreement, clashes and conflicts. This kind of God will be increasingly denied by the intellectual and it will not be very long before educated people of future generations will have eliminated God from their hearts altogether. Even now those who are educated, though they may use the word God occasionally, they use it mostly from habit only. It comes out in times of war or in important affairs. Even in laboratories the name of God may be used when a scientist fails to prove something further, or finds results or problems that he cannot explain because the causes are not known. Such a God is only a God of the lips, a word out of habit in the form of exclamation, but no true God. This type of God can be found in every religion and in every language. To believe in ghosts, in spirits, angels, fortune, fate, and so on, is the manifold appearance of belief in this kind of God, or we might say that these things turn into God for such people. If this situation continues, then that which is called God will have less and less real meaning and in the end there will be nothing left but superstitious beliefs and practices. This is the problem of people who hold to the concept of God as a person in the conventional sense of the word.

To understand God we must progress from the lower levels of understanding to the higher, until we understand God in terms of Dhamma, not in terms of man, mind, or spirit (viññāna), but in terms of something special which has no body, no heart or mind, no form, and is not under the power of time or space, something which cannot be explained by conventional language, but which must be explained in terms of religious language of the kind that is used in highly competent religious circles. If this can be done then the thing which we call God will be acceptable to intellectuals and can surely dwell with man in a way that will not cause conflicts, but will truly rule the world. As for the word God in conventional terminology, leave it for children or for those who cannot yet understand God according to religious terminology, until such time as they reach the stage where they can understand it. To sum up this point: God as generally thought of, is the God of conventional language and is not the God of religious language. The word God as we use it really refers to two levels of concepts or the two meanings as we have stated.

For the convenience of our further comparison we will now state clearly these two definitions: The God of conventional language is the God to whom is ascribed some sort of body, a God who loves, who becomes angry, who wants this or that, who can do both good and bad and so forth. As for the God of religious language, he does not have a body, does not occupy any place, does not love, does not get angry, is above all desire, does neither wrong nor right. However, it may be said that the God according to conventional language can be so interpreted as to mean the God of religious language in every respect. But the problem is whether believers in a personal God are able to understand this changed meaning. *If they can't, then their God is still a God for children, or for people who are only beginning to learn and there is no way for them to approach the real God as can be done by a person of higher intelligence and wisdom.* There is no way for them to arrive at that goal which is the goal of the Bible or of any other religion. So you can see how important it is that we should study the real meaning of God according to religious language and that we should put forth every effort to this end.

Another thing which we should notice and understand and which is just as important is this: Every religion has something that can be called God, but there are some religions that talk about God in terms of religious language only. It appears, therefore, that those religions have no God and they are then classed as atheistic religions. Buddhism and Jainism are such religions. Another group of religions mostly uses easily understandable conventional language when talking about God, and they are then classed as theistic religions. Christianity, Hinduism and Islam are such religions. These religions however, have much to say about God in terms of religious language, which is very profound, but which is buried deep under the outer shell or form of these religions. *The classification of religions into two groups, atheistic and theistic, is a very shallow classification and does not touch the real essence or meaning of religion.* The reason they are so classified is because people in general are only able to understand things in a shallow way and thus are unable to get down to the heart of religion. Consequently they come to despise religion more and more. And especially they despise God. Finally some of such people declare that they have no religion and they feel proud to be atheists.

I shall now speak about 'God' as found in Buddhism, in order to show the characteristics of "God in terms of religious language."

2. GOD IN TERMS OF RELIGIOUS LANGUAGE FROM THE BUDDHIST VIEWPOINT

God as creator is known in Buddhism under the term '*avijjā*'. This means the lack of knowledge, ignorance.

Ignorance is the power of nature which is the cause of all existing things and as such the cause of suffering.

God as repenting that he had created the world (as is found in Genesis 6/6, 7) is known in Buddhism as '*vijjā*' or knowledge opposed to the ignorance of not realizing that the creation of anything is the creation of suffering itself.

God as controller of the world, who punishes or rewards creatures, is known in Buddhism by the word Karma (or Kamma) or the Law of Karma. The Law of Karma controls all creatures living in the world.

God as destroyer of the world is known in Buddhism under the name '*vijjā*', knowledge in its capacity to bring all suffering to a final end.

God as omnipresent witnessing all that man does, is again known in Buddhism as Karma or the Law of Karma.

However, it should be noted that all these things, i.e. ignorance, knowledge and Karma are all included in the single term Dhamma. Moreover, such things as kindness, beauty, justice, truth, etc., all of which can be thought of as being God's or parts of God, are all included in Dhamma, Dhamma being all-inclusive. Therefore, Dhamma is God. There are four aspects of Dhamma: 1. Dhamma as the nature of things (SABHĀVADHAMMA), 2. Dhamma as the Law of Nature (SACCADHAMMA), 3. Dhamma as duty performed according to the Law of Nature (PATIPATTIDHAMMA or NIYYĀNIKADHAMMA), and 4. Dhamma as fruits of practice, or of realization (VIPĀ-

KADHAMMA or PATIVEDHADHAMMA). All these four are altogether called Dhamma. Here the second aspect of Dhamma *(The Law of Nature)* can be seen easily as standing directly in the position of God. But equally the other three also stand in the position of God as shown below and must be respected and honoured in every way.

The *Dhamma as nature* is something that God created, or to put it in another way, it is the (result of the) will of God. We must respect and honour and take an interest in it in order to realize the truths of nature. To realize the truths of nature is, in a way of speaking, to attain to God. In other words, realization of the truths of nature enables us to accept without resentment the so-called will of God even though it appears in such forms as floods, earthquakes, plague and even death. The nature in the garb of different natural phenomena manifests the will of God better than anything else and *in fact all natural phenomena constitute the very God.*

As for the *Dhamma as duty*, we should respect it by practising it strictly and this is the same as abiding by the will of God strictly in order to attain to God. This attempt to do one's duty to the utmost is the true supplication to God that is not person; but even if God were a person he would surely want attendance to duty rather than mere words of supplication coming only from the mouth.

Now the *Dhamma as results*, or good fruits which man should receive should be honoured in a way that in

Christian usage is called *Thanksgiving for the grace of God*. This grace of God refers to the highest thing that man can receive. To earnestly desire for this thing is in itself to show great respect for God. This kind of respect has more meaning than any bodily postures or words uttered according to custom to glorify God.

These four things (altogether called Dhamma) are, in one way or another, the aspects of *'God in true religious language'*. Some people may wonder *how it can be that that which has no feeling like man can be called God*. But when one considers carefully, it will be seen that *this kind of thing is more properly called God than anything with feelings like a person*. For God to have feelings like a person would mean that he would have feelings of love, of anger, etc. A God of this kind is under the authority of man who can make him angry. He is not stable. He has form and is therefore under the power of time and space. All of these qualities would make God into a being like an ordinary person. This is what gives rise to the term *'God in the language of common man'* which is a very low God. But in Christianity there is God in the sense of religious language, as decribed above. It is called the *'Word'* as appears in John 1/1,2 where it is said: "*In the beginning was the Word, and the Word was with God, and the Word was God*". The term 'Word' here means the Law of nature and it is correct to say that it is with God and that it is God. *When the 'Word' is God then is it not possible for the Dhamma to be God?* In reality they are one and the same thing for they are there before anything else. Similar words are found in

Buddhism: "*DHAMMO HAVE PATURAHOSI PUBBE*"— meaning "*The Dhamma indeed appeared before*" (Kāliṅgavaggavaṇṇanā, Jātakaṭṭhakathā). The word 'God' signifies power and the term 'Word' signifies Law. *As for the term 'Dhamma', it refers to both the power and the Law and comprehends much more than this.* It is a very strange term and cannot be translated into any other language.

In order to understand *Dhamma* better we might draw a parallel between the four aspects of Dhamma and four Christian conceptions.

> Dhamma as nature = this world with its living creatures
> Dhamma as the Law of nature = God
> Dhamma as duty = religion as system or practice
> Dhamma as fruit or result = Consummation or Salvation

Thus we can see that these four things even in Christianity can be included in the one word Dhamma. It also becomes clear here how the term 'Dhamma' has a much wider meaning than the term 'God'.

The Dhamma in its four aspects can be found completely in the man or in the life of man. Thus says the Buddha: "*The world, the cause of world, the cessation of the world, and the way to the cessation of the world—all these things I have shown to be found in this fathom-long body complete with perception and mind*" (Rohitassa-sutta, Catukkanipāta, Aṅguttara-Nikāya). The so-called world here *refers to the world of sin and suffering as it also appears in the Christian Bible.* The world amounts to creation, the cause of the world amounts to creator, the cessation amounts to consummation and the way to the cessation amounts to redemption. All these are included again in the one word Dhamma. Dhamma here has been used in the sense of God as mentioned above. To put the whole matter in another way, the world itself is the will of God. The cessation of the world is the final will of God and the way to the cessation of the world is the act of God in helping the creatures of the world. So all these four things are God either directly or indirectly and cannot be otherwise. *Thus God in this sense is also God in Buddhist terms of religious language.* This God can be met with within this life by any one who has wisdom and who is sufficiently trained.

Buddhists hold that the *Dhamma implies everything* and that God being perfect also implies everything. This is because Dhamma and God are one and the same thing. Buddhists also hold that the so-called devil or Satan is included in the word 'Dhamma' or God, because if God had not created Satan what could have created him? The devil or Satan is nothing else but a test of man by God. We can say that there is nothing that has not come from the Dhamma or from God—which term is used depends upon how we were taught to label things or how we were brought up. The question may arise: "Why is it that you call that which God created, 'God'?" The answer is: "Because it is just included in that which we call God". Let me clear up this point further:

If things of nature such as earth, water, fire, air, etc. were not already in God from where would God get these things to create this so-called universe? If there were anything else apart from God then God would not be perfect. Therefore, nature itself is included in the word God and there is also to be found Satan or the Devil, call it what you may. So we can see that the so-called God is what in Buddhism we call, 'Dhamma'.

As for the Law of nature it is easy to see that it is included in the concept of God. If God did not have, or was not himself, the power which we call the law of nature, then whence would he get that power to create and control all the things? God is to be feared because he is in himself the very law of nature. Buddhism calls the law of nature Dhamma, in the sense of the natural order of things.

As for the duty of man according to the law of nature, that is directly the duty of God. The law of nature requires duty (according to itself). If God does not have the duty, *or is not himself the natural duty*, how can he help, love, or punish man? And from whom will man learn examples of different ways of the practice and the performance of various duties? So the function of helping the world is one more aspect or part of God. It is a function which has been turned over to man to be performed as his natural duty. To take God in this sense and respect him, or hold onto him as such (as duty), is to do the will of God in the best sense. Again, Buddhists call this duty Dhamma as we have already mentioned.

Finally the fruit that we receive according to the law of nature, or consummation, is also included in the word 'God'. If this were not the case, then what would

God take and from where would he take it, to give to man in return for doing *his will*? If there is some part of nature from which he takes it, which is not God himself, then God himself is not complete and fails as God. Buddhists also call this fruit of practice, 'Dhamma'. Though they may give it different names such as fruition, supermundane Dhamma, realization, and so on, ultimately it all comes down to one word 'Dhamma'.

We may sum this up by saying that the Dhamma includes all these four things, i.e. nature, the law of nature, the requirements or duties according to the law of nature and the fruits which come about according to the law of nature. Thus it is complete in itself even as that which is called God by others, is complete in itself. God in the religious language of Buddhism then has those four characteristics. It is a way of explaining God by reaching back behind the facade of the person to the inmost nature of the truth (Dhamma) which lies behind the person. To use the conventional mode of expression, there are beings who have both body and mind, or spirit. Then it is held that there are beings who have only body (Asaññībrahma) and there are beings who have only mind or spirit (Arūpabrahma). If God is explained in these terms, it is personalism (Puggalādhiṭṭhāna) i.e., God is reduced to a personal entity, or it is personification of God. It is speaking in conventional language rather than in religious language. We should realize that personification (puggalādhiṭṭhāna) is a figurative way of speech, or ordinary language used by common people who know nothing of the Dhamma. What is expressed by such language is not the ultimate truth as is expressed in religious language. So God, in the religious language of Buddhism is neither a person, nor spirit, nor body alone, nor is it both mind and body together. But it is nature which is impersonal, devoid of any self, It has no attributes, has no form or size. It is not under the power of time and space. It is not possible to say whether it is one or many, for it is beyond the concept of counting or measuring—yet it really exists and it is the fusion or unification of all the countless different things, with their different meanings, powers and functions. *God as a person in the sense of conventional language, when compared to the God of religious language, is like a single speck of dust compared to the whole universe.* God in terms of religious language is 'immeasurable'. If God is a 'person' or spirit, then it is something finite and measurable by standards of one kind or the other. Body and spirit are but drops in the ocean as compared with God in terms of religious language. Therefore Buddhists do not hold that that which is called God is 'spirit'. It is Dhamma or Nature in the sense of something non-constituent, unconditioned or uncompounded (Asaṅkhata-Dhamma). Words fail to precisely express its characteristics (in positive terms).

To put in negative terms, *Asaṅkhata-Dhamma* has no birth, no stay and no death. It cannot be said to be good or evil. There is no cause that accounts for its existence. It has no like or dislike for the actions of anyone. It does not hear the supplications or prayers of anybody. It is not moved by prayers. It has no form for it takes up no space and it has nothing to do with time. It gives nothing to anyone and receives nothing from anyone. These are only a few of the innumerable characteristics (in negative terms). It is immovable, unchangeable, and perfect in all respects. It is all-inclusive and therefore omnipresent. There is another type of Dhamma, or nature in the sense of something conditioned, constituent or compounded *(Saṅkhata-Dhamma)*. It refers to such things as matter, body, mind, spirit, action and result of action, which having come into being cease to be. They are called natural phenomena of the world. They are illusory. They spring from ignorance. It is the very ignorance which is ceaselessly creating these illusions. Out of illusion, these natural phenomena are ascribed the innumerable dual qualities of good and evil, happiness and suffering, man and woman, etc. *But the essence of these phenomena is not thus* (the dual qualities), and *this is* the state of their being uncompounded (Asaṅkhata-Dhamma) which is hidden in all the phenomena and cannot be seen in the ordinary way. And it is because of inability to see the essence that people grasp at the changing shadow as real and consequently suffer.

The law of nature is *Asankhata* in the sense of its being impersonal. *It is active in everything, in every atom of everything perceptible to the eyes, ears, nose, tongue, touch-receptors and mind.* It is also found in every action and reaction of these things. This state of Asaṅkhata-Dhamma, both as something *hidden* in everything and as *active* in terms of the law of of Karma (or of nature) should be seen by means of religious practice. To see it is to see God. To see it is to slough off illusion. To see it is to live with God or live without suffering. *To live without suffering is to live in the Kingdom of God.* The long and short of it is, that the misconception of 'I' or 'self' is destroyed and with its destruction suffering is destroyed, for, suffering results from the grasping of 'self'. But when it is put in terms of the language of common man it is called entering into the Kingdom of God.

All the aforementioned four aspects of Dhamma (i.e. nature, the law of nature, the duty and fruits) are *Asaṅkhata Dhamma* in the sense that they are impersonal, having nothing to do with anybody apart from their being as such. It is the hidden nature of all these things. This is the Dhamma which is equivalent to God in the religious language of Buddhism.

The word Dhamma is also used for the teaching of the Buddha. In this sense it is very much used in school textbooks and refers to all the recorded sayings of the Lord Buddha. The teaching of the Buddha deals with all the aspects of the Dhamma which should be studied and followed to attain to the '*Dhamma*' which implies God according to religious language. Apart from these meanings there are still other meanings of the word Dhamma much as in the Christian religion the God has many meanings, such as Son, Spirit, etc. However, those who practise and have realized the nature of these things will come to the one and the same thing in the end.

Having examined the meaning of the word God in religious language we should also discuss the term 'God' according to its conventional usage in order to see how this usage has given rise to various difficult problems.

3. "GOD" AS USED IN CONVENTIONAL LANGUAGE

The word 'God' used in conventional language has been the source of many difficult problems which arise in regard to the correct interpretation of the word. If it is incorrectly interpreted, or is not interpreted at all, it cannot accord with or go with the various fields of knowledge. In that case it requires blind faith. It is because of its wrong interpretation that people give up their religion and embrace a new one, or have no religion at all. It is also the cause of friction between members of different religions.

I hope you will pardon me if I give an illustration which is rather coarse. Suppose we tell a child that God is omnipresent, or is in everything. And if the child immediately asks: 'Even in a dog or in dog excrement?' Then how will we answer? The child knows the word God only in the conventional meaning of the term and so cannot understand how God could be in such things. Yet if we say he is not in them, that is even worse because *if God is not everywhere then he is not God.*

God in conventional language refers to God as a personality with emotions like man, such as anger and love. He cannot be in such things as excrement because they are dirty and smelly. They are too low for the highest to dwell in or to have anything to do with. As for God in the sense of Dhamma, that is, the law of Karma, the law of cause and effect, the law of creation and destruction and so on, he is impersonal, having no feeling as man. This kind of God knows no cleanliness, no dirtiness. Therefore this God can be in everything, even in dog excrement.

Here we should say something about certain terms that some Buddhist sects use. They are: Buddha-nature (Buddhabhāva), voidness or emptiness (Suññatā), suchness or thusness (Tathatā), etc. They are applicable to everything including dog excrement. This is simply because these terms do not have reference to a person. The word Buddha in *Buddhabhāva* implies voidness (meaning absense of a self) of the person called 'Buddha'. The Buddha-nature is but 'Dhamma' or a reality characterized as different stages of development of *knowledge*. Here *knowledge* signifies understanding of *voidness* of 'I' or 'self' at different levels. Development of this knowledge is comparable to the germination of seed into a full-fledged tree. It (Buddhabhāva) may be in latent or dormant state like ungerminated seed or may be beginning to sprout, or growing up, or fully-grown as in a man who has attained enlightenment. Each stage of this development can be called the *Buddha-nature*. Each stage has equally the characteristics of voidness or emptiness. It is hidden deep and cannot be taken by appearance or seen on the surface. The Buddha says: " He who sees the Dhamma sees me " (Itivuttaka, Khuddaka-Nikāya). It means that he who sees only the person of Buddha has not really seen him. Only when he has seen the true Dhamma, which is in the Buddha's body and is in everything including his own body, only then can it be said that he has seen the Buddha in a way that the Buddha would approve. So he who has seen the body of the Buddha has seen him only in the conventional meaning of the word 'see', but he who has seen the Dhamma has seen the Buddha according to the religious meaning of the word 'see', and it is the true Buddha that he has seen. That the Buddha, according to the meaning of conventional language, should be in every place at all time is obviously impossible. *But the Buddha, in the religious meaning of the term, can be everywhere at all time.* Just in the same way, Dhamma in the sense of God, can be in every place even in the excrement of a dog, in its capacity as the law of Karma, the law of cause and effect, and the law of impermanence. So, to put it in other words, God in conventional language is simply a word which is used when speaking to children. Or it is used by grown-up people who, being intellectually immature, feel and think like children. They will use the word 'God' in that way until they are intellectually matured enough to understand, as it were, the meaning of '*God*' according to religious language.

The Bible is full of references to God in the sense of conventional language. In the Bible there is no orthodox or official interpretation of God in religious language. One is first told to believe in God according to the literal or conventional meaning, until later one comes to understanding of the real meaning of 'God' by oneself. Therefore it is but natural that in due course of time there should be revolt against the 'belief' since some people cannot be forced to believe for a long time. It might be that to interpret God in terms of the religious language would not be suitable in that age and at that place because, far from being appealing, it would hurt the feeling of people in those days, who believed in the holiness of things. But in this present age, things have changed and we should now interpret every sentence and every word in terms of religious language. I believe that there are some words that are the cause of much confusion and that have caused many problems among religions. Especially it is very true of the word *'Spirit'*. Christians say that the true God is not a man or a person but is Spirit which is translated as *chit* or *winyan* in Thai (derived from *citta* and *viññāṇa* in Pāli language). The word 'winyan' in Thai or 'viññāṇa' in Pāli simply means something that is not enduring. It is brought into existence by certain conditions. It is constantly changing and is only one of the several aggregates of life-process. Therefore Buddhist cannot understand God in terms of Spirit (chit or winyan). When Buddhists read in the Book of Genesis that God who created the world had the characteristics of a person, with feeling and thoughts like a person, they wonder how a God like that can be called *winyan* or *chit*. And when they hear the word *'Holy Ghost'* used for God, they cannot understand at all. It becomes all the more difficult for them to understand God. Therefore, all such words should clearly and precisely be defined or interpreted according to religious language. This is imperative so that Buddhists can understand Christianity and work together without friction or persecution for the common good. According to Buddhists God cannot be, or have, a *personality* or *individuality* because God is no person and has no characteristic by which we may say that God is like this or like that. Even the conceptions of monotheism or polytheism cannot be applied to God.

Such a thing which is devoid of any characteristics is designated as Dhamma or nature by Buddhists. It is the common noun which, unlike *chit* or *winyan*, can be universally used for anything whatsoever. So in my opinion the usual connotation of the word '*winyan*' is a barrier for understanding of God. Spirit can be taken as God, but it would be God in the language of common man. It cannot be true God of the religious or Dharmic language. I think that God as spoken of everywhere in the Bible can always be understood in religious or *Dharmic language.*

4. GOD ALWAYS CONVEYS A HIDDEN DHARMIC SENSE. THE IDEA IS THAT GOD, AS SPOKEN OF IN THE LAYMAN'S LANGUAGE, WHEREEVER FOUND IN THE SCRIPTURES OF ANY RELIGION, COULD BE TURNED USUALLY INTO THE SENSE OF THE DHARMIC GOD. To save time, I shall quote an example from Genesis dealing with God's creation.

God's creation as described from Chapter I to Chapter 3, was creation with regard to the spiritual (Dharmic) side, as known to Buddhists. This implies that man, in the process of evolution, developed his mental faculty, from the stage of a low animal to a higher stage whereby he was no more considered an animal. That is to say, he became a real man both in the physical and spiritual sense. Human civilization established itself in the mind of an animal whose body, prior to that time, assumed human shape but whose mentality was still on a level with that of a beast. According to scientific theory, man in physical structure is believed to have appeared approximately two hundred thousand years ago, whereas the age of our physical world is not less than a billion years. Calculating from what has been said in the Bible, *the creation of the world could have taken place in* roughly eight to ten thousand years. Hence, the created "world" referred to in Genesis could not possibly be applied to the material or physical world but must necessarily point out the meta-physical world or the Dharmic world which pertains to the spirit or the soul. What seems strange, is that some authorities in Christianity still do not allow their members to believe that man came from an ape-man which again evolved from an ape. This has certainly led to confusion. Such a belief is, perhaps, quite correct, but it applies to what happened millions and millions of years in the past and not to man who appeared about ten thousand years ago. The "created world" therefore could have only meant the spiritual world, or, in the Dharmic language, a well-developed world in the mind of a person who was so refined as to set himself apart from an animal. This idea fits in with the sense of the word "man", (manusya in Thai and Sanskrit) which, whether it is to be translated *as a descendant of the Lord Manu* or *even as a well—cultured animal,* will be found acceptable to the Buddhists, by virtue of this saying of Lord Buddha: *"The world, its cause, its annihilation, the path towards its annihilation—all these are declared by the Tathāgata as being complete in this fathom long body, inclusive of perception and mind."* (Rohitassa Sutta Catukka-Nipāta, Anguttara-Nikāya). This clearly explains that the Dharmic or religious "world" is applied to the *"world within the mind of man"* and not to the world of physical matter which is the world in the ordinary sense, or the world outside man. *A true God should be concerned with the creation of the inner world within human consciousness to deserve the title of God.* Had He been busy with the creation of the material world or a world of the flesh, He would have degraded Himself down to an absolutely meaningless God. Even in His concern with the creation of animal and matter, He would have had to be more particular with the part of the spirit such as consciousness, and the law of Karma, (cause and effect) which are also latent in these things. We may call it the spirit or the soul of such things, no matter what they are — may it be only a small particle like gravel or a stone. God is so mysterious a Power, beyond the description of the human tongue, able to create and control everything definitively; how-be-it, the text dealing with the creation of man as appearing in Genesis, still directly refers to the creation of human spirit which is Dharmic in sense and may be seen from the following details.

In Genesis 3/24, we are told how *God failed in forbidding man to take the fruit of the tree of knowledge of good and evil* and how He succeeded in preventing him from taking the fruit of the tree of life. This means that, prior to that time, man had lacked human consciousness in so much as being unable to distinguish good from evil, male from female, the clothed from the naked, and husband from wife. We know that such knowledge was also not possessed by an ape-man. Even in normal sexual intercourse between the male and female, the attitude of being husband and wife did not creep in as it did with man in the age of "taking the fruit of the knowledge of good and evil". *Because of the very discretion man owned as a result of his being so developed in mind,* he has prided himself as a perfect man, which has consequently raised in him still more conflicts concerning good and evil, so much so that it has given rise to another kind of suffering which is solely with man and is not found in animal. This is exactly the death penalty which man deserved from God as a result of his taking the forbidden fruit. Man has burdened himself with the task of having to tackle his life-problem regarding birth, growth, decay and death, which is due to his failing to take the fruit of another tree known as the tree of life whose fruit of Immortality would have given man an everlasting life — as everlasting as God Himself.

In the Thai version of the Bible, the "tree of life" is translated as "the tree of prosperous life", which, in my opinion, falls short of the original sense. It should be translated precisely as "life" which in itself means "not dying"; for life is what does not die. The moment man has taken the fruit of this tree, he will not die, that is, he will secure the wisdom known in Buddhism as "*Amata-Dhamma*" — the Deathless State, or the seeing of Non-self. Thus, there is nothing which can die, be born, grow old and get sick. In a way, he is said to attain the Arahantship in Buddhism, which is characterized by certain expressions such as Gaining the Deathless or Entering the Great Immortal City, that is, Attaining Nirvana within this very life-time as consciously felt by an individual. The Genesis also contains what we call in

Buddhism the Lokuttara-Dhamma or Amata-Dhamma. If the translation of the Bible is done correctly in Thai, the Buddhists will surely hold as great a love and a high reverence for the Bible as they do for their Tripiṭaka. For this reason, a new and careful revision of the Bible in the Thai language is recommended. The term "prosperous life" according to Buddhist concepts involves a never-ending series of still more refined and more subtle forms of suffering. To put it precisely, "life" would refer to another kind of life known in Dhamma as the Eternal life which Christ often talked of in his discourses and which is known in Buddhism as "Amata-Dhamma" or as Eternity or Immortality.

What I have so far said, is sufficient to show that whether it is the word "God", or "the World", or "the tree of the knowledge of good and evil", or "the tree of life" — all these can be given a Dharmic sense apart from the literal meaning. Such a rendering is necessary to enable one to get into the substantial meaning of these words. Then one will see that Christianity has also presented a sublime form of Truth on the Ultramundane plane as Buddhism and as other religions of like Dharmic principles, and is not a mere "ancient Hebrew tale" as it is called by some. Further details that deserve our attention (rendered into the Dharmic language) can be seen from the following extracts.

Genesis 1/26, reads: "And God said, Let us make man in Our image, after Our likeness---". These words have brought another deriding factor. Some Christian text books, even competent ones, have asserted, with all available reasons, that God is formless. Those children to whom I have given these books do not believe this, for the Bible has clearly said that God and man have the same likeness, this "by the will of God". This results from the wrong interpretation of the word in the Dharmic language. That man was created after God's own likeness should be taken to mean that man's vast capability can be in the same state as God or be in unity with Him; that is, if man has taken the fruit of the tree of life he will become a God. God has only postponed that chance for the time being, as was made known in Genesis 3/24. He gave special protection to that tree in order to turn man away from it. To argue about God in respect of His bodily form or His physical aspect is senseless.

In Genesis 2/7 we find: "And the Lord God formed man of the dust of the ground, and breathed into his nostrils the breath of life; and man become a living soul." "The man of the dust of the ground" here refers to man in the remote past who, despite his possession of a human body, nevertheless lacked human consciousness. He was a dumb animal, no better than an earthen structure in human form. Down to the period when he had undergone certain developments which enabled him to distinguish himself from all the other animals, God was then said to breathe into nostrils the breath of life. This act can be taken as another new creation—the creation of the spirit or the mind which is the reason for our belief that the creation of the world must be one with regard to the creation of the spirit.

In Genesis 2/21-22 we read: "And the Lord God caused a deep sleep to fall upon Aam, and he slept; and He took one of his ribs, and closed up the flesh instead thereof. And the rib, which the Lord God had taken from man, made he a woman, and brought her unto the man."

No one would be willing to accept the above passage as it is written, without expecting a concealed meaning, and one worth looking for. From the Buddhist viewpoint, it conveys the idea that woman has not got the same right and function as man. This is supported by another statement in Genesis 6/2 which calls man "son of God" and woman "daughter of man" — an inference to show that man and woman are not equal. Man was created from earth, a symbol of strength of character and that is why he is called "man", whereas woman was but a part of his body and hence called "woman" which means part of a man. Man ranks himself as the son of God but woman is just the daughter of man; so how can the two be equal both in their rights and their functions? It should be borne in mind that God (or nature) did not intend man and woman to possess the same likeness and the same potentiality. A woman will have to bear children and feed them from her breast. The attempt in our modern days to assign to both sexes the same office is striving against the will of God or blindly going against nature. Should any woman intend to become a man, she is advised to go for an operation on her glands and replace them with those of the male so that she will become a full man. That would look much better than deceiving others by putting on an outward show while retaining her inward nature. At the same time it will not be against the law of God. All this so far serves to affirm that Christianity like Buddhism has not recognized woman in the same measure as man regarding her right and function. Lord Buddha said: "It is not possible for woman to become a Buddha but it is quite possible for a man to become so". (Aṭṭhānapāli, Ekakanipāta, Aṅguttara - Nikāya). There are also other sayings which speak of the inappropriateness on the part of a woman in case she should become an Empress or a Brahma. In the Catukka - Nipāta, Aṅguttara - Nikāya we again find words showing Lord Buddha's approval of certain customs observed by women in India of that time which demanded that woman should not sit in parliament; should not take up highly - specialized work; should not go to the country of Kamboja (compared to the going abroad for study at the present time), accompanied by the reasons why that should be so, which can be summed up by saying that woman is not composed of the required calibre — both in physique and in will - power. For nature has created woman with an object quite apart from that of man. Should she replace man in his role, her duty on earth will not be fulfilled and consequently many new problems will arise. This is none other than God's punishment inflicted upon mankind. We may conclude that the Biblical narrative which recounts man as being created from earth and woman as being a product of man is definitely correct and quite natural indeed. Should we fail to understand this, we may take it for granted that it was written for us to become fools. It should not be looked upon as an absurdity or as a mere "ancient Hebrew tale".

In Genesis 2/16-17 we also find: "And the Lord God commanded the man, saying, of every tree of the garden thou mayest freely eat. But of the tree of the Knowledge of good and evil, thou shalt not eat of it: for in the day that thou eatest thereof, thou shalt surely die." If the foregoing text is to be taken literally and with a blindfolded attitude, it will look very clumsy. None will understand why God should have spoken thus. God created man and loved him most tenderly. Why should it be against His will to see man growing up with knowledge? We have got to dig out the underlying sense, deeply conveyed in the ordinary language before we can understand its real meaning. It can be simplified by this explanation. Any suffering that arises in man is a result of his getting attached to what is considered good and evil. Sometimes he is so harassed by feelings of dislike of evil that he dare not put his hand to anything. Sometimes he is so occupied with the thoughts of doing good as to be unable to sleep at night. Some go so far as to commit suicide to escape being accused. This attachment to good and evil generates desire and craving and illusion which rate as suffering itself. It may also account for the all-round growth of greed, anger and delusion which causes man to suffer. As soon as man rids himself of the attachment to good and evil, releases himself from the idea of virtue and sin and lives entirely beyond the conception of good and evil, he is said to attain Arahatship or the State of Nirvāṇa according to the Buddhist principles. That God forbade man to take the fruit of the tree of the knowledge of good and evil should not be taken as His lack of mercy in leaving man as a brute. On the contrary, it was rather His kindess to keep man away from his contact with the root-cause of suffering which, in a way, is equivalent to spiritual death. That is why God said: "For in the day thou eatest thereof, thou shalt surely die" which can be explained as follows. In any period when man begins to conceive of good and evil and to hold attachment for it, he will encounter at once a new form of suffering, worse than all the others which may be held identical with a spiritual death. This eventually turns into another life-riddle which needs to be remedied first and foremost and with a great effort. It is quite correct to consider the taking of the forbidden fruit as man's original sin, since it was at this time that he first slipped into the abyss of sin which has sullied him through countless generations. Some may not agree that the sin of the first man has been passed on to posterity if sin is meant for the individual. In fact it reflects how man in the past, had already initiated imperfections of the most subtle form which have been handed down to the present by continually imparting that delusion to one another quite unconsciously. If this were to be the Dharmic interpretation of the above text, original sin in Christianity could then be understood, and this viewpoint could also be shared by the Buddhists as being the same as the Noble Truth of Buddhism, that is, to hold an attachment to neither good nor evil as it brings unavoidable suffering.

Although the tree of life, whose fruit could render man immortal, may not receive any direct mention afterwards, yet in a way it had been fully treated by the very words of Christ whenever he dealt with the Path towards Eternal life which could be compared to the taking of the fruit of the tree of life — a thing so dear to God as to be the cause of their (Adam and Eve's) fall from the garden. However, in the end Christ had widened the opportunity, during his life-time to the progeny of Adam to partake of that fruit. Buddhism may not have offered such an analogy, but it has concentrated on the observing of the Dharmic principles aiming at the elimination of all kinds of attachment. At this stage, one is said to have attained the Amata-Dhamma or the State of Immortality which lifts one up above all concerns with the problem of death. In this sight, there is none to be born and none to die. There exists only one Infinite State that may be termed "Dhamma" or "God", forever clear in one's consciousness. This is the Dharmic interpretation of "the forbidden fruit" thereby putting Christianity in conformity with Buddhism.

The last example is to be found in the words of Genesis Chap. 6/5-6-7 which run as follows: "And God saw that the wickedness of man was great on the earth, and that every imagination of the thoughts of his heart was continually evil. And it repented the Lord that He had made man on the earth, and it grieved Him at His heart. And the Lord said, I will destroy man whom I have created from the face of the earth; both man and beast, and the creeping things, and the fowls of the air; for it repenteth me that I have made them."

If the above context is to be put into the Dharmic sense, it can be understood in many ways, such as, God can also make a mistake. This accounts for the fact that in God there is everything, including wisdom and ignorance. Any creation is to be taken as an act of ignorance whereas thinking of dissolution and non-creation is wisdom. In any event, we cannot conceive of God as a person capable of getting angry, grieved or pleased. That would certainly be a mistake, for it is clearly stated that God will destroy even "the creeping thing" and "the fowls of the air" which were in fact not guilty of any wrong. So God's repentence in this case should be positively applied to the actual feeling of a person so highly developed in mind as to realize that any sort of creation is to be pitied, and abhorred. To refrain from creating tends towards calmness of mind. Thus the dissolution of the desire to create is no other than the annihilation of the growth of the "self". Man of this aspiration will hold a detestable feeling for the cycles of rebirth or the wheel of becoming, known as *Vatta-Saṁsāra*. All that has so far been propounded serves to reflect God's awareness on the part of wisdom that is the knowledge to abstain from any desire to create. However, in the end, God had not actually destroyed the world as was literally said in the Bible, because that is just a Dharmic expression in the same sense as when it speaks of Adam that he would succumb immediately if he took the forbidden fruit but actually Adam did not die. Hence the word "destruction of the world" is a figurative way of representing man's true realization of the misery brought about by his desire to create. But people in general, by force of habitual craving, could not hold back from such tendencies and consequently have to bear the miseries like their followers. The loathesome attitude towards any desire to create is likened to the dawn of Lokuttara Dhamma or the Super-mundane Dhamma in the mind of man which will gradually bear fruit in him in the future. That sublime feeling is equated to God acting as human wisdom. The Dharmic principles of the Buddhists have also encouraged such observances as will lead towards the procurement of said wisdom, and will finally bring man to a state of Non-becoming or Nirvana.

By His very essence, a true God is above what we call right and wrong, although both notions are to be found wholly complete in Him. That God cannot be said to be either good or evil inspite of His full possession of the two, is because such terms as "good" and "evil", "right" and "wrong" are conceptions formed by men and are not attributable to God. For God, such conceptions are without sense. An epidemic and a peaceful living have equally the same meaning in the sight of God and are treated as a single entity. But for human beings these mean a great disparity; men will look at them with varied attitudes so as to prefer the one and turn away from its opposite. For such reason, it is rightly said that a calamity like a flood, a fire or a plague or its absence, even life and death and several other pairs of opposites are all equally the will of God. There is not a shade of difference between them for Him. As for men, those who have not yet attained Godhood—who have not yet been at one with Him, will not tolerate the evil consequences. They will choose only what is agreeable and will shun its opposite. Those alone who have truly absorbed themselves in God or Dhamma will not view them as opposite and will treat them as equally meaningless. Nor will they have feelings of like or dislike for either. To say that God is pleased or angry is only an expression in the lay language which has got to be rendered into the Dharmic language almost in this manner. As soon as one can grasp the correct meaning, one will begin to like God, to feel attached to Him, to worship Him with an unfailing love and will finally admit that God is the Most Supreme of all things, there is nothing higher and that is what is known by the word "Dhamma" in Buddhism. He may be called by other names in other religions such as 'Tao' in Taoism which also carries the same purport.

It can thus be summed up that God and all about Him in whatever relations, that are described in the layman's language can always be rendered into the Dharmic language. This would bring about a real benefit and pre-eminent success to people in the world only when the Dharmic sense has been perfectly grasped. That we sometimes call God "the Father" or "the Primary Cause" for instance is due to the fact that God is the sum-total as well as the outlet of all things both worldly and unworldly. It looks as if He were simultaneously the Creator and the Destroyer of the world when taken in the literal sense. The word "world" here no less refers to non-physical world or the world of delusion within the frame of human mind which is Dharmic in nature but is employed in ordinary usage.

From now on, we are going to consider God the son which refers to Jesus Christ, as being the preacher of his Father's words and also the redeemer of mankind at the expense of his own life in order that man will release himself from original sin and will in the end come unto God or the Eternal life.

5. GOD THE SON

As the Son, Jesus Christ may be considered in four different lights: 1. as a Son of David, 2. as a prophet, 3. as the Son of God and 4. as God himself. The first two aspects have to do with his apostleship, while the other two are dharmic in significance.

The life-story of Jesus Christ is depicted in the Bible by group of writers who were his disciples. There is not a single autobiography in the Bible. This may be because of his short time on earth (as Christ), a mere three years—too brief to record anything much beyond short sketches. It may also be due to the absence of any efforts to compile his teachings right after his death as in Buddhism. In the Tripitaka (the Buddist Bible), there are quite a number of occasions where Lord Buddha is found to be telling his own story generally from his childhood to his Nirvāṇa. His biograpy would fill a book of the size of the New Testament. We must therefore satisfy ourselves with whatever life-story we can find from the writings of Matthew, Mark, Luke and John, all of which makes up just one half of the New Testament. The four aspects of the Son will then be discussed on the basis of these four books.

(a) Jesus as a son of David

This is his physical state, much in the same way as the Lord Buddha being the son of King Suddhodana, and has little dharmic value. Jesus himself discounts the significance of this relationship when he reported by Matthew (12/49) and Mark (3/34) as saying: "For whosoever shall do the will of my Father which is in heaven, the same is my brother and sister and mother". Hence the attempt to trace the genealogical relationship back to David, an ancestor of Joseph, who is not his true father any way, must have been of later fabrication in order to enhance Jesus family status. On the other hand, that very attempt appeared to be a blasphemous negation that he is the Son of God, as may be deduced from the Bible. Similarly, to call the Lord Buddha by his genealogical name as the "Samaṇa Gotama" would be a degradation. It seems that Jesus was referred to as a son of David for the first time in Matthew 9/27 by the two blind men who sought a cure for their blindness. If these two blind men believed that Jesus could restore their sight in the capacity of the Son of God, why then would they refer to him as a son of David ? This would then lead us to believe that the part concerning David's son must have been of later addition, perhaps at the time when the need was felt to ennoble his pedigree on earth. In the same way, we also find later biographies of the Lord Buddha such as the Pathamasambodhi (a book written by a Thai monk) where his pedigree was traced back to King Sammatiraja, the first king on earth, although no mention of this is to be found in the Buddhist sayings, nor even in the Tripitaka at all.

It must be conceded that biographies of teachers are somewhat exaggerated. Nevertheless, we have developed the habit of accepting such exaggerations thereby perpetuating such beliefs from generation to generation.

(b) Jesus Christ as the Prophet

The term "prophet" has also been applied to Jesus Christ in his own words as quoted by Matthew 13/57: "A prophet is not without honour save in his own country and in his own house". Similarly, Lord Buddha is also recognized as one of the religious teachers. Some even refer to the Buddha as a pagan, as distinguished from heathens when referring to outsiders. In the Thai language, pagan is applied to all outsiders, as if we don't have a pagan among ourselves. Therefore, even though Jesus may be considered a pagan, he is by no means degraded by the term. A religious teacher or a prophet also belongs to a pagan class. The reason I mention this is that there are some ignorant Buddhists who refer to Jesus as a pagan in a degrading sense.

That a prophet is not honoured except in foreign lands is but natural. Even Lord Buddha had encountered hostile reactions from his kinsfolk. He was never exactly honoured by them as by the outsiders. Some of his relatives stood firm in denying him any respects even in his glorious days.

As regards has perfect prophethood, we read in Matthew 28/18: "And Jesus came and spoked unto them. All power is given unto me in heaven and on earth". From the Buddhist's point of view, Jesus has triumphed both in his mission and as an individual. As a person, he is not bound to this world or to things mundane. In his mission, he succeeded in converting others by placing his life at stake. In other words, he had survived all kinds of entanglements whatsoever in the Buddhist sense of the word. "O Bhikkhus," said Lord Buddha "I am now free from all sorts of shackles, be they divine or human and all of you are free from all shackles too, be they divine and human." He aims at ultimate victory above anything else. We might therefore say that one of the most important features in a prophet is, they all are victors. We Buddhists regard Jesus as one of the victors.

As regards Jesus method of propagation, it is surprising to note that he proceeded in the same manner as practised in India five centuries ago, despite the distance between his native land and India. Jesus used parables to get his points across in his Sermon of the Mount and so did Lao Tsu in Tao Teh Ching. The parable of the sower of seeds mentioned in Matthew 13/3-9 very much resembels the sayings of Lord Buddha. Take for instance, "They that mourn are happy, they that hunger are contented, and they that are persecuted are blessed." (Matthew 5/4-6-10). Very much the same thing appears in Buddha's sayings. And just as Jesus, Buddha also gave such startling injunctions such as "Kill thy father and thy mother", "Be thou ungrateful" (DHAMMAPADA) These statements have special meaning by themselves, for they are similes in the Dharmic language.

The Christian principle of kindness as taught by Christ in Matthew 5/39 - 40: "But I say unto you, that ye resist not evil; but whosover shall smite thee on thy right cheek, turn to him on other also and if any man will sue thee at the law and take away thy coat, let him have thy cloak too", represents the highest form of forbearance. The counter-part in Buddhism is Lord Buddha's saying: "Hadst thou been captured by a robber, who cutteth thy flesh with a saw unto thy bones and thy bones unto the marrow, and should any of thee, O Bhikkhus, feel even as much as the least enmity towards the robber, thou art not of me." Let any one compare these two statements in all their subtleties. It is safe to imply that these two religious are the religions of mercy. It is pity that religious men in modern days have again succumbed to the law "an eye for an eye and a tooth for a tooth". That is why the world is constantly harassed by wars and crisis of enduring permanence. As far as human relations are concerned, this injunction of mercy is one of the most neglected.

Even in ordination rites, ironically enough, both Jesus Christ and Lord Buddha taught the same principles. Buddha's call of "Ehi Bhikkhu" (Come, monk) is parallel to Mark 1/17 "Come ye after me," or to "follow me" as said to the Levi in Mark 2/14. This indeed is all that is needed to become ordained a monk, calling the novice to perform an act which would rid him of all sufferings. The elaborate rites of ordaining as practised later were never prescribed by Lord Buddha. This may seem too trifling to mention, but the coincidence is quite amusing to note.

I would now like to say something about miracles.

Miracles have always been the most baffling issue in all religions. For those in constant fear, who have not quite grasped the Dhamma yet, miracles must of course be resorted to, otherwise they would never pay any attention to religion at all. A miracle simply means anything so astoundingly wonderful as to capture the hearts of men, and does not just include anything so weird or fantastic as to defy all attempts at explanation. *Even a common act like a persuasion which has convinced a man against his former convictions, may rightly be spoken of as a miracle.* The Lord Buddha himself had made use of, and has recommended to others to make use of this sort of miracle. He disapproves of, and has forbidden, the use of witchcarft or other supernatural means, which, he points out, can be performed by any magician. Had Lord Buddha resorted to magic, he could have easily been regarded as one of the magicians, just like Jesus who, upon having expelled the devils, had become known as owing his success to the Prince of the devils, rather than as the son of God.

Such miraculous phenomena as causing the blind to see, the deaf to hear, the dumb to talk, the paralytic to walk, the tiger or the lion to befriend the lamb, were said to be comtemporary occurences at the time of Lord Buddha's Enlightenment, according to the writings handed down to us, such as the NIDĀNAKATHĀ of the JĀTAKA-AṬṬHAKATHĀ. Nevertheless Buddhists generally ascribe to such phenomena a moralistic (dharmic) sense. For instance, by *"causing the blind to see,"* we interpret blindness as ignorance, so that the Lord Buddha, by virtue of his being enlightened and thus ridding himself of ignorance or blindness, has also prescribed a remedy for the world to follow. The world has thus been *saved from blindness when the way becomes clear or the means to eliminate sufferings becomes understood.* Again, "causing the deaf to hear" may be taken to mean to simplify the hitherto incomprehensible concept of NIRVĀṆA for all to hear. "*To cause the paralytic to walk*" is to give guidance to the world so as to stand up and walk its way across the pitfalls of suffering. "*To restore speech to the dumb*" is to teach the world how to express Dhamma intelligently. Finally, "*to cause the lion to befriend the lamb*" is to create peaceful co-existence through the power of mercy amidst the strong and the weak alike. It is only when such miraculous phenomena are viewed from the dharmic standpoint that we may begin to believe in the miracles and their wonderful effects. Between one who can cure a blind man, and one who can dispel ignorance in a man, who is the superior in his miraculous act? Whose work is more wonderful? Or more difficult? Hence, in Buddhism, the miracle of teaching (anusāsanī pāṭihāriya), which makes one realize the immortal Dhamma is regarded as far *superior to other sorts of miracles.* Even if the dead are brought back to life, what good would it do if men are as ignorant and as susceptible to all kinds of sufferings as they were before their deaths? To raise the dead to life should properly signify the raising of one who had died as a result of Adam's having partaken of the forbidden fruit, to a new life in which he would attain the

Kingdom of God. I think this must be what the Bible means when it says that Jesus restored life to the dead. Unfortunately, this significance was too refined for the Pharisees to grasp, hence they plotted against Jesus' life.

With all his miracles having proved in vain among the Pharisees, Jesus Christ therefore ceased to perform them further, lest their disbelief might grow sevenfold. Matthew (12/43-45) reported Christ's words as follows: "When the unclean is gone out of a man he walketh through dry places, seeking rest, and findeth none. Then he saith I will return into my house from whence I came out; and when he is come, he findeth it empty, swept, and garnished. Then goeth he, and taketh with himself seven other spirits more wicked than himself, and they enter in and dwell there: and the last state of that man is worse than the first. Even so shall it be also unto this wicked generation". Jesus Christ found it fruitless to perform miracles to the Pharisees. Not only in vain did Christ try to convince them, but also he was accused as invoking the help of the prince of the devils (Matthew 12/24).

From Matthew 12/41 and 16/4, we may deduce that the greatest of miracles performed by Jesus Christ consisted of his resurrection on the third day following his death. Again, we must interpret this in the dharmic sense. "Three days after Christ's death" may be regarded as a certain length of time, be it three years, thirty years, or three hundred years, following which his teachings would again "come to life". Similarly, Buddhism came to life in the third century after Lord Buddha's death, i.e. during the time of King Ashoka the Great, the upholder and propagator of Buddhism. Again we may consider the prophecy stated in later writings that a time will come when the bone-relics of Lord Buddha which are scattered all over the world will reunite and he himself will become alive once again, his teachings will become even more glorious, and he will thereafter pass into Nirvāna perfectly. The idea of a religious teacher coming back to life had been prevalent *among the Indians even before the time of Lord Buddha.* This idea, like the "ancient lores of the Hebrews", must be taken in the dharmic sense. Whether the former adapts the idea from the latter or vice versa is a subject for further research. *We may however conclude that what is considered miraculous, whether in Buddhism or in Christianity, presented in fairy-tales for children or childlike adults must be reinterpreted in the dharmic sense, otherwise it would only make us seven times more ignorant as if seven more devils have entered our spirit.*

Let us now consider the story of the *treacherous disciples.* Jesus Christ had his Judas Iscariot, and Lord Buddha, his Prince Devadatta.

Strangely enough, both Jesus Christ (John 6/64-70) and Lord Buddha knew beforehand that some of their disciples would betray them. Why then did they admit these would-be traitors into their fold? Judas is known to have been picked out by Jesus himself. The reason must be stated in dharmic terms. Of course it would be possible to say, in the case of Jesus Christ, that *it was the will of God for the redemption of man* through charitable deeds even unto those who were known to be the most wicked. In the case of Lord Buddha, the betrayal was considered a natural event on Prince Devadatta's part, and had made no difference to one who had already freed himself from illusions, Lord Buddha just let *things happen in their course*. To him there was no question of betrayal or loyalty, for he had no desire whatsoever, be it for gain, loss, life or death. In terms of redemption, to admit a traitor into his fold is one way to attract the people's attention to his teachings, his sacrifices, and his guidance that they might also attain success. Incidently, it may be safely stated that all religious teachers faced betrayal, not just Lord Buddha and Jesus Christ; the differences lay only in the degree and circumstances of the betrayal each one had encountered.

(c) Jesus Christ a Son of God

Those who disbelieve in Jesus Christ might look down on him as an illegitimate child without a father. In Matthew 1/20 we read: "But while he (Joseph) thought on these things, behold, the angel of the Lord appeared unto thee Mary thy wife: for that which is conceived in her is of the Holy Ghost. And she shall bring forth a son, and thou shalt call his name Jesus: for he shall save his people from their sins." Literally, this might signify that Jesus Christ is the Son of God. Similar significance is found in Lord Buddha's biography which was discovered at Bharhuta in stone inscriptions of the 4th century B.E:- " A white elephant descended from heaven ", says the inscription, "hovered thrice around Queen Mahamaya and then entered her womb. This happened during the period when Princess Mother was keeping the Observance day Precepts (UPOSATHA-SĪLA), pure from the touch of any man, and deep in dream." Other writings, such as the Paṭhamasambodhi, also contain the same episode. Therefore the belief that a religious teacher must be born of God, and not of mortal beings, *was quite common in India one or two centuries before the birth of Jesus*. If one more teacher, Jesus, claimed to have been born of God, the Buddhists (and Hindus) would not be surprised at all for they can recall that similar births had occurred in India already. It depends on how we are going to interpret this event.

In the dharmic sense, *to be the son of God can mean many things*. Jesus Christ, for instance, may be considered one of the different components of God, sent to guide the world along with the other teachers who formed other parts of God from time to time. What is known as "God" is neither physical nor spiritual in nature, it is bodiless, without mouth, without any faculty of speech that we know of, but it can cause a body to be formed, with a mouth and a voice to speak what God wishes him to speak. That speaker may therefore be called the son of God. In Mahayāna Buddhism, it is believed that a particular Buddha called "Ādi Buddha" exists in eternity, as much as is generally referred to God. From Ādi Buddha came the various historical Buddhas, such as the Gotama Buddha, Jesus etc., each having appeared at a different time according to circumstances. The concepts are undoubtedly parallel. If you agree that God is "the Dhamma" then we can safely say that *Dhamma is the womb of everybody* including the prophets or the teachers. The difference is that most people do not speak about what "the Dhamma" requires in order to obtain salvation. What most common people speak generally results in sufferings or encouraging sin. Hence the term "son of God" cannot be applied to all, but only to those who can lead the world to perfect understanding of the dhamma.

But whether the son of God is personal or dharmic, Buddhists are prepared to accept him without argument.

(d) Jesus Christ as God Himself

The New Testament contains suggestions that Jesus Christ also possesses heavenly messengers and kingdom. This might show that Jesus Christ is here referred to as God Himself. We might reason, for instance, that in Jesus Christ is godhood. His body contains the soul of God, and that soul is endowed with the attributes of qualitative faculties of God. When referring to Christ, should we point at refer to his physical body or his soul? Lord Buddha says: "He who sees the Dhamma sees us; he who sees not the Dhamma, sees us not, even as he be holding our robes." (Itivuttaka, Khuddaka - Nikāya). This means that those who see the Buddha are those who see the *Dhamma in his mind*, not just his body or his mind only. For that which lies in his mind, is the Dhamma or God. That thing therefore is not just a son of God or anything else, but the God himself. "Buddha" is the "Dhamma", and "Dhamma" is the God. Jesus Christ, insofar as what lies in his soul, is no less than God Himself. The body and the soul are just receptacles or outer shells. Hence, Jesus Christ as a God himself may be acceptable in this line of reasoning.

Hence, Jesus Christ in his fourfold role as a son of David, a historical teacher of religion, a son of God and God, may then be understood in the same way as we Buddhists are familiar with our Lord Buddha.

6. God the Spirit or God the Soul

Before proceeding with my discussion of God in the form of a Spirit or soul, may I once again draw your attention to John 1/1-5 in the New Testament:

"1. In the beginning was the Word, and the Word was with God, and the Word was God.

2. The same was in the beginning with God.

3. All things were made by Him; and without Him was not any thing made that was made.

4. In Him was life; and the life was the light of men.

5. And the light shineth in darkness; and the darkness comprehended it not."

What then is 'the Word'? *I think the Word is what may be referred to as the Spirit*, which has been rendered into Thai by 'the Holy *Ghost*' or 'the Soul'. Such rendition has caused a great deal of misunderstanding among the Thai readers. The 'Spirit' being thus wrongly conceived, the concept of God the Spirit must consequently be also misunderstood. God has therefore been taken in the sense of consciousness or soul. "The Word" signifies Life and Light as clearly shown in the above passage. What we call the Spirit comprehends Life and Light in full measure. Hence it cannot be the equivalent of 'the Holy Ghost' or 'the Soul' as rendered in Thai, unless these two words are defined to reflect the special meaning not present in the ordinary sense of the words in Thai, or even in Pali from which these two words are derived.

Obviously, "the Word" is no other than the Dhamma in the sense of Natural Laws, or what is known in Buddhism as the Truth (SACCADHAMMA). In the beginning was the Truth; the Truth was with God; the Truth was the life and the light of men. Hence it is the Spirit or the essence of everything. In Buddhism what forms the essence of everything is termed as Dhamma—there is no word better than that. Hence the Spirit and the Buddhist Dhamma are naturally equivalent. The Dhamma is both life and light at the same time. Etymologists might examine the roots of the word 'Spirit' in Latin and Greek, so that the Thai version can be more accurately produced, both literally and meaningfully. This is one of the most important terms in Christianity since it represents God. The effort would be worthwhile because *it would give the Thai readers a better idea of what the Spirit or the Soul is*, so as to readily accept it as God without any qualms. As for the word 'Holy *Ghost*', the Thai people have never been able to understand this. They shudder at the word 'Holy **Ghost**'. Perhaps it might help us to see the point more clearly if we examine the three words in their combination — the Trinity.

7. God the Trinity

In order to explain the Trinity to a child, we might use such analogies in the language of the layman as follows:

The Father in Heaven may be thought of as the owner of an enormously vast quarry of gems.

The Son — Jesus Christ — is the man who brings forth the gems for distribution to all mankind.

The Spirit (or the Soul) represents those gems.

These three are one. They all have gems in common. Their functions are in unision and inseparable. They resemble the Buddhist Trinity—the Buddha, the Dhamma, and the Sangha.

The Buddha discovers an immense resource of gems.

The Dhamma is all the gems that exist.

The Sangha brings the gems to the whole world.

Thus defined, let anyone see for oneself the relationship between the Trinity of the Buddhist and that of the Christian. Where then is the difference? The most essential step to take is to render the word 'Spirit' as applied to God into a more appropriate word in Thai which would reflect the original word in Hebrew, Latin or Greek sources.

The Trinity, viewed from this angle, would enable Christians and the Buddhists to work together side by side in a way that has never been possible before.

To summarize this second lecture, I maintain that in order to attain to Godhood, *one must first meticulously examine one's concept of God*. This will enable one to know the real God in the Dharmic sense and enjoy the company of God for successively longer periods until one lives with God, without leaving his company even for a moment. The result of this would be the same as that of realization of the Dhamma by the Buddhist, that is, making the mind clean, clear and calm.

God as generally understood is something which *demands faith and commands awe and supplications. One must creep into the good graces of God by way of doing his will.* But God in the Dharmic language of Buddhism involves analysis in terms of Ignorance, Knowledge, the Law of Karma and so on. Ignorance (AVIJJĀ) or craving *(TANHĀ* — the active counterpart of AVIJJĀ) accounts for the creation (of the world of suffering) and Knowledge (VIJJĀ) or wisdom accounts for its destruction which results in peacefulness. God as the Law of Karma is to be seen in the performance of action culminating in the end of both good and bad Karma. The end of good and bad Karma is to bring the cycle or wheel of becoming to a standstill, which refers to the very state of peacefulness.

God in conventional language is intended for people with childish ideas or childish way of thinking and therefore the garb of mythology has been used in order to make such people easily remember and believe in things pertaining to *"God"*. God in the mythological sense can always be interpreted in the language of the Dhamma. And it is imperative, too, to do so, otherwise people will fail to know the real God and remain stuck in the mire of superstitious belief.

God the Son, i.e. Jesus Christ, whether in the sense of a son of David, or a historical Teacher or the Son of God, or even as an embodiment of perfection, has strangely enough a career in resembling that of Lord Buddha.

God the Spirit should be viewed as the NIYYĀNIKA-DHAMMA of Buddism as the best gift to mankind, the spiritual gem which is the most gratifying. The concept of God the Trinity is common to all religions known to man in some form or the other.

THOMPSON MEMORIAL LECTURE

Fifth Series

by

THE VENERABLE BHIKKHU BUDDHADĀSA INDAPAÑÑO

Third Lecture

REDEMPTION AND CONSUMMATION

Members of the Faculty, Students and Guests of the Seminary:

In this third part of my talk, we shall consider a couple of concepts known as "*Redemption*" and "*Ultimate Consummation*".

(1) REDEMPTION

Buddhists have the impression that *the redemption effected by Jesus Christ* corresponds to "*the development of Perfections in order to remove man-kind from all sufferings*". Prior to becoming perfectly Enlightened, a person must develop Perfections for the sake of others, even to the extent of sacrificing his life, his beloved son and wife, his limbs, his vision, everything he owns. Even after becoming a Buddha, He still goes on *to remove* mankind's sufferings, which may be likened to hell-on-earth. He thus brings about a blissful calmness in the world even unto its dumb animals. Such an act directly involves the sacrifice of one's life or personal happiness in service of other men, and therefore be termed "*Redemption*", that is, applying self-sacrifice to redeem mankind from the entanglements of defilements or cravings. Man is possessed by ignorance, which, like a creditor or the devil, holds man in his grip. In terms of Dharmic language, man is buried in his own folly, utterly blind, and refuses to listen to anyone who would teach him. Hence there needs to be someone who is prepared to sacrifice even his own life in order to wake man from his folly and to save him from sufferings which he himself cannot perceive. The sacrifice of life by a *"Redeemer"* has an everlasting effect, for He leaves His discourses as an inheritance for the world, and these are taught for centuries after He has passed away.

The fundamental significance of " Redemption " which must be correctly grasped is its two-fold or double-layered character. The first layer is *the redemption of other people* and the second, *self-redemption*. It was necessary for Lord Buddha to make every sacrifice in order to find a way to get rid of mental defilement or to kill the Mara (the evil one). He then sacrificed Himself by embarking on the task of preaching to mankind in the midst of grave dangers until He finally won their hearts. Once the Buddha's preaching has been understood and practised so as to free oneself from one's own ignorance and defilements, one is thus saved. The first redemption is by the Lord Buddha, and the second, by the person himself. There are the two stages of redemption. The most essential part lies in the latter stage. Hence Buddhists regard self-redemption as a cardinal principle, to the extent that it is prescribed: "Attā Hi Attano Nātho" i.e. "*Self is the refuge of self*" (Attavagga Dh. Kh.) The Lord Buddha

Himself advocated this principle, saying: "You yourself must make the journey. The Tathāgatas can only show the way" (Dh. Kh. 25/51). Without making the journey by oneself, one can never reach the "Kingdom of God".

Nevertheless, *without the Buddha to show the way, there would not be any journey at all.* Even if someone found the right path, after striving hard, he would not be able to come back to pick up his fellowmen. His knowledge would be too narrow in scope, and could only be used for his own good. He would be at a loss to convince others of the profound truth he had found. It takes someone who is endowed with the virtues of a Buddha to succeed in showing the way, so that later generations may follow in his foot steps. The primary Redeemer is therefore the Enlightened Teacher and the real redeemer is no other than the traveller himself. If this concept is acceptable, we can then see that redemption is common to all religions, identical in essence, and differing only in minor details.

Redemption and Atonement are two different concepts. Atonement for sins is effected through the medium of another person, and belongs to the realm of supernatural phenomena. No explanation is offered. In Hinduism, for example, there is an episode of Rama atoning for the sins of Ahalya. It does not convey the meaning of redemption as herein propounded, unless its significance in the language of the layman is converted to that of the Dharmic. Buddhism does not believe in atonement through supernatural means or objects such sa the holy water. It believes in redemption but only in the sense mentioned above.

As regards the question: "What kind of redemption should be regarded as the "Great Redemption", the Buddhists do not regard how much or what has been sacrificed as the criteria, but rather what the redeemed has obtained thereby. This means that if redemption has resulted in the highest good to man—such as leading them to Nirvana or the Kingdom of God, such redemption is to be considered the "Great Redemption", regardless as to whether the life has been sacrificed to secure such an end or not. If a life has been sacrificed without appreciable results, it is lost in vain, and can never be understood as the Great Redemption. The Greatest Redemption to be achieved is not necessarily at the cost of the redeemer's life.

To me, the title of the "Great Redeemer" has been conferred on Jesus Christ because of His efforts in directing the children of Adam who, having partaken of the fruit which had caused Adam's spiritual death and which has been passed on to his progeny in the form of original sin, turn back and partake of the fruits from the "tree of life" once again and rid themselves of the original sin; in other words, to practise what Jesus Christ has taught so as to be able to enter into the Kingdom of God. For this, Jesus came to be known as the Great Redeemer and not because of His crucifixion. For a person like Jesus Christ or Lord Buddha, life is too insignificant a thing to cling to. But then I have observed that a great many Christians hold to the idea of redemption as exclusively the sacrifice of Jesus life. I therefore wish to present the views of the Buddhists in the way of a comparison. I would like to say that whether Jesus Christ did or did not sacrifice His life is incidental to natural circumstances, and may have nothing to do with redemption whatsoever. Had He preached in India, especially in an era contemporary with that of the Lord Buddha, He might not have been forced into paying with His life and might have been able to continue preaching. Christ's highest form of redemption consisted in His being able to lead men unto the Kingdom of God through consummation. If He were to talk to fools, He would never be able to convince them no matter how many lives He was prepared to sacrifice, for, none would reach the Kingdom of God.

The true meaning of redemption is merely the "Resurrection" referred to in John 3/3 which represents what Jesus Christ would have most wished. The Lord Buddha defied Aṅgulimāla's scimitar and resurrected him there and then. This is an example of the highest form of personal redemption according to Buddhism. We may therefore define redemption briefly as "to cause man to be reborn spiritually in this very life on earth". Every religion embodies redemption as an essential course of action and without this, would have no significance.

Going one step further, we may say that redemption of sin is an act of Loving Kindness (Mettā). One must possess the highest form of Loving Kindness in order to be able to effect redemption Even if we were to say that redemption was effected at God's will, it must have been from the God of Loving Kindness — an attribute of God.

In lay language, God out of His Loving Kindness sacrificed His own son in order to redeem mankind from its sins. Since man naturally loves his own person, he may therefore redeem himself as well. He may do so by employing the methods preached by the Teacher i.e. following His teachings in all respects, and thus fulfilling God's will. I therefore maintain that to redeem man is the duty of every religion, and at the same time it is the duty of every man to redeem himself. To redeem oneself is possible even through the power of instinct (i.e. power from within, not without), for all living beings instinctively desire security. The only difference for man lies in security (safety) through religion which is the highest form of security. This, however, would be greatly facilitated if instinct were allowed to play its part.

Men, with no religion or knowledge of religion, who are endowed with normal intellects, also strive for their security in some way or another. The fundamental aim may be the same in that they wish to be spared the sufferings which are torturing their mind. The moment they begin to seek a way to conquer sufferings, they immediately profess a "religion" unconsciously, and are thus engaged in redeeming themselves. This psychological fact accounts for the success of the teachers in redeeming the people of the world. If people were not intent on redeeming themselves, no amount of sacrifice by the teachers would result in their redemption. We should therefore agree that redemption in a religious sense is based on the instinct for security at different levels, on the part of living beings. If religious institutions realize the full importance of this instinct of security, efforts at redemption would bring about happy consequences, and the world would become a far more worthwhile place in which to live.

All mankind must co-operate with God towards self-redemption. All must bring about "resurrection" by practising the principles of religions which are there to be studied and observed until they are thoroughly understood and then earnestly applied to life. This is what we call "to sacrifice one's life to God", which would then agree with God's will to help us — this is to use the mixed terms of the lay language and that of Dhamma. But, in fact, we must love ourselves, help ourselves and have to overcome all evils by ourselves in order to be free from all kinds of sufferings. By doing so, we shall be entirely redeemed from the "original sins", or "new sins" or the "present sins".

Concerning the manner of redemption, i.e. the line of practice for redemption, though religious scriptures may differ in their wording, the essence remains the same. In Christianity, for example, mention is made of sacrificing oneself in the service of God, or serving one's fellowmen in order to serve God, behaving oneself as a relative of Jesus Christ in the way he would have wished etc. In Buddhism, the same thing may be found; "Keep making merits or doing good", "eliminate ignorance", "free the minds from all attachments" and finally "perform acts which are neither virtuous nor evil and thus be above both good and bad". Literally these my be different, the one always mentioning God, the other not even a trace of Him. But in essence both are the same.

Even if we were to use the terms "pray to God", it could still signify self-pursuasion to do God's will. Doing God's will is practising the Dhamma, and to practise the Dhamma is to eliminate selfishness, which is common to all religions. All sins spring from selfishness. Selfishness is the cause of greed, hatred and misunderstanding. It is selfishness which is responsible for evoking sinful deeds bodily, verbally or mentally. We redeem all these sins by practising their antidotes. This is much the same as eliminating darkness by lighting a lamp. This way of behaving (destroying selfishness) is indeed "praying to God", for we try to please Him by complying with His will.

As regards the words of prayer, these are but a kind of self-persuasion or praying to ourselves to act according to God's will, for the words used in prayers tend to motivate us towards goodness, or towards the path leading to God. Without abhorrence Buddhists can come to an understanding as regards the prayers of any religion, provided that the wording is interpreted in terms of Dharmic language. This is true even for the prayer of the Bahai religion which runs as follow:

>May thy Beauty be Divine Food for my feeling;
>May thy Presence be an Elixir to my heart;
>May thy Pleasure be my entire hope;
>May the remembrance of thee be my companion in the journey;
>May thy Abode be mine.

For, by substituting "Dhamma" of "Thy", the whole prayer becomes a Buddhist principle. Please give some thought to this. It is not at all difficult to understand. The Buddhists also have a kind of prayer. They pray to the Buddha, the Dhamma, and the Sangha for "forgiveness" of their transgressions, each morning and evening; but in the Dharmic language, for the purpose of self-direction or self-persuasion, not to do wrong in the future. Of course, there may be some who view such prayers in a literal sense due to their insufficient education. This is natural and is common to other religions as well. Buddhists who are well educated would "pray to Him" by their practical deeds.

To summarize, redemption of mankind began with the teachers, who made great sacrifices for mankind's sake, and fulfilled our response in trying to understand their teachings. Whether the redemption is great or not depends on the worth of what we have achieved thereby. Collective redemption of sins in this manner is the essence of every religion, for it will purify the earth, and free it from all kinds of sufferings. This is the common objective of man's religions.

(2) CONSUMMATION

The ultimate consummation that man may derive from religion is *his happiness in this world and the good things that he may enjoy in the future world of God.*

The good things in this world, such as wealth, fame, social recognition and a peaceful family life, may be accredited to general cultural standards or cultural values and may not necessarily have anything to do with religion. The great cultures of the world have emerged out of religion, although perhaps in *a rather primitive form*. Hence, *the direct benefits obtained through religion* have had to do with things in another world beyond the scope of human cultures. That world is generally known as the *Kingdom of God*.

The Kingdom of God has different meanings. In the layman's language, it means the world to be obtained after death. But in the Dharmic language, the Kingdom of God, in reality, means the world existing within this world itself; which *common people fail to see*.

Furthermore, the laymen speak of the world of God as full of beautiful, gratifying, fascinating objects, but in greater quantity than in this world, better in quality and more heart-robbing. But in Dharmic language, there are no such things. It is, in fact, a state of mind which is peaceful, tranquil, and free from all struggles, delusion, intoxication and worries resulting from desire to possess those fascinating objects in their dream-land. The taste of this peacefulnesss is more satisfactory, more fascinating than all of the things fancied by the layman. The Buddhists call this state of condition "Nirvāṇa", which may be attained in the world here and now. It is this state which is called the *Kingdom of God. And mankind must strive to accomplish the journey before it dies a natural death.*

Concerning this kind of peacefulness, the most interesting advice contained in the Bible is found in Corinthians, 7/29-31 teaching the way of life characterized by freedom from all attachments: "......they that have wives be as though they had none; and they that weep, as though they wept not; and they that rejoice, as though they rejoiced not; and they that buy, as though they possessed not; and they that use this world, as not using it......". In Buddhism, this is known as "*freeing one's mind from attachment in terms of "I" or "my"*, which is imperative to put into practice in our day-to-day lives. Each time that our minds are stimulated through the eyes, ears, nose, tongue, skin, or imagination, we must be able to control it in order to prevent the mind from arousing egoism or selfishness in ourselves and thus live a life of perfect wisdom and serenity. As long as we live peacefully in this way, so long will we live in the *Kingdom of God, for during this time there is purity, light of wisdom, peacefulness and serenity beyond all description. Only then will we be able to work for our own benefit and for the good of others.*

We also find that *Jesus Christ admired a state of mind, like that of an innocent child,* as may be read from Matthew 19/14 and 18/3-6. So much so that Jesus Christ has come to be known as "lover of children". This is because the mind of a child does not cling to its body or its possession as much as the mind of an adult and is therefore not burdened with so many sinful thoughts. In short, it does not become so attached to anything as *to bring sorrow to itself.* Therefore, if these two Biblical concepts are well understood, you will see for yourself that *Christianity and Buddhism have more things in common than you have ever known, thought or hoped.*

Another amusing point common to both religions is that *the best thing in religion is to be given free.* In

Matthew 10/9, one reads: "...... freely ye have received, freely give". In Revelation 21/6 ".... I will give unto him that is athirst of the fountain of the water of life freely". And in Revelation 22/17 "..... And let him that is athirst come. And whosoever will, let him take the water of life freely". In Buddhism, it has been said: "Laddhā Mudhā Nibbutiṁ Bhuñjamānā" that is, they are enjoying *Nirvana which has been attained for nothing, freely.* (Ratanasuttra, Khuddakapāṭha, Khuddaka - Nikāya). All this shows that *the loftiest thing of God is obtained freely.* But seekers must strive to obtain that with perseverance, as mentioned in Matthew 11/12 that: "....... the Kingdom of heaven suffereth violence, and the violent take it by force". This struggle can be seen to be more violent than the hunt for the gold mines of jewel pits of the world. It is a great pity that not many people appreciate this and do not persevere in their struggle to obtain it.

    Thus, *the ultimate consummation of religion sought by man,* is what is called *the loftiest Dhamma* or the Highest Good or Summun Bonum that man can attain in his lifetime, not after his death. Provided that a person is not spiritually dead like other common people who die many times during a single day by being victimized by evil or ills (suffering), as soon as he puts God's words into practice, that kind of death will not touch him. He will be born anew, enjoying the life which knows no such death. In Christian terms this is called *"the entry into the Kingdom of God"*, and in Buddhist Dharmic terms, *"the attainment of the Deathless"*, and to use the layman-language, "*the entry into the land of Nirvāṇa*". *Is this possible in this very life or is one to wait for it in one's grave ?.* Let the wise think and decide for themselves.

Summary of the three lectures

Clear understanding of religions should be promoted because that is what God's will is. Each person must be tolerant towards all others, for even in one's own religion, one has hardly grasped the whole truth. We are indulging too much in studying the text-books rather than about what God really wants. We are not putting religion into practice in proportion to our studies. "God" in Christianity is what is known as "Dhamma" in the fourfold sense in Buddhism. In "This Thing", there are all the duties that need to be taken care of, and we hardly need worry about anything else. Once one has grasped the concept of "Dhamma", one becomes a good Buddhist, a good Christian and a good Muslim all at once. Creation, Redemption and Consummation once interpreted in terms of Dhamma, from the point of view of Buddhists, would leave no room for disagreement between religions.

Printed By: MitrNara Printing
              Tel. 392-0146   Fax: 381-0238

ABOUT THE AUTHOR

Buddhadāsa Bhikkhu (Slave of the Buddha) went forth as a *bhikkhu* (Buddhist monk) in 1926, at the age of twenty. After a few years of study in Bangkok, he was inspired to live close with nature in order to investigate the Buddha-Dhamma. Thus, he established Suan Mokkhabalārāma (The Grove of the Power of Liberation) in 1932, near his hometown. At that time, it was the only Forest Dhamma Center and one of the few places dedicated to *vipassanā* (mental cultivation leading to "seeing clearly" into reality) in Southern Thailand. Word of Buddhadāsa Bhikkhu, his work, and Suan Mokkh spread over the years so that now they are easily described as "one of the most influential events of Buddhist history in Siam." Here, we can only mention some of the more interesting services he has rendered Buddhism.

Ajahn Buddhadāsa has worked painstakingly to establish and explain the correct and essential principles of original Buddhism. That work is based in extensive research of the Pali texts (Canon and commentary), especially of the Buddha's Discourses *(sutta piṭaka),* followed by personal experiment and practice with these teachings. Then he has taught whatever he can say truly quenches *dukkha*. His goal has been to produce a complete set of references for present and future research and practice. His approach has been always scientific, straightforward, and practical.

Although his formal education only went as far as seventh grade and beginning Pali studies, he has been given five Honorary Doctorates by Thai universities. His books, both written and transcribed from talks, fill a room at the National Library and influence all serious Thai Buddhists.

Progressive elements in Thai society, especially the young, have been inspired by his teaching and selfless example. Since the 1960's, activists and thinkers in areas such as education, social welfare, and rural development have drawn upon his teaching and advice.

Since the founding of Suan Mokkh, he has studied all schools of Buddhism, as well as the major religious traditions. This interest is practical rather than scholarly. He seeks to unite all genuinely religious people in order to work together to help free humanity by destroying selfishness. This broad-mindedness has won him friends and students from around the world, including Christians, Muslims, Hindus, and Sikhs.

Now he focuses his energies on his last project, establishing an International Dhamma Hermitage. This addition to Suan Mokkh is intended to provide facilities for:

— courses which introduce friends, foreign and Thai, to the natural truth explained in the Buddha's teachings and start them in the Buddha's system of mental cultivation
— gatherings of representatives from the different religious communities of Thailand (and later the world) in order to meet, develop mutual good understanding, and cooperate for the sake of world peace
— meetings among Buddhists from around the world to discuss and agree upon the "Heart of Buddhism"

The ultimate mission in Ajahn Buddhadāsa's life can be summed up in his Three Resolutions, posted at the entrance of Suan Mokkh:
1. To help everyone to realize the essence of their own religion.
2. To help develop mutual understanding between all religions.
3. To help to drag the world out of materialism.